I0436278

Editor-in-Chief and Founder:
   Lyndon H. LaRouche, Jr.
Editorial Board: *Lyndon H. LaRouche, Jr. , Helga
   Zepp-LaRouche, Robert Ingraham, Tony
   Papert, Gerald Rose, Dennis Small, Jeffrey
   Steinberg, William Wertz*
Co-Editors: *Robert Ingraham, Tony Papert*
Managing Editor: *Nancy Spannaus*
Technology: *Marsha Freeman*
Books: *Katherine Notley*
Ebooks: *Richard Burden*
Graphics: *Alan Yue*
Photos: *Stuart Lewis*
Circulation Manager: *Stanley Ezrol*

INTELLIGENCE DIRECTORS
Counterintelligence: *Jeffrey Steinberg, Michele
   Steinberg*
Economics: *John Hoefle, Marcia Merry Baker,
   Paul Gallagher*
History: *Anton Chaitkin*
Ibero-America: *Dennis Small*
Russia and Eastern Europe: *Rachel Douglas*
United States: *Debra Freeman*

INTERNATIONAL BUREAUS
Bogotá: *Miriam Redondo*
Berlin: *Rainer Apel*
Copenhagen: *Tom Gillesberg*
Houston: *Harley Schlanger*
Lima: *Sara Madueño*
Melbourne: *Robert Barwick*
Mexico City: *Gerardo Castilleja Chávez*
New Delhi: *Ramtanu Maitra*
Paris: *Christine Bierre*
Stockholm: *Ulf Sandmark*
United Nations, N.Y.C.: *Leni Rubinstein*
Washington, D.C.: *William Jones*
Wiesbaden: *Göran Haglund*

ON THE WEB
e-mail: eirns@larouchepub.com
www.larouchepub.com
www.executiveintelligencereview.com
www.larouchepub.com/eiw
Webmaster: *John Sigerson*
Assistant Webmaster: *George Hollis*
Editor, Arabic-language edition: *Hussein Askary*

EIR (ISSN 0273-6314) *is published weekly
(50 issues), by EIR News Service, Inc.,
P.O. Box 17390, Washington, D.C. 20041-0390.
(703) 777-9451*

European Headquarters: E.I.R. GmbH, Postfach
Bahnstrasse 9a, D-65205, Wiesbaden, Germany
Tel: 49-611-73650
Homepage: http://www.eirna.com
e-mail: eirna@eirna.com
Director: Georg Neudecker

Montreal, Canada: 514-461-1557

Denmark: EIR - Danmark, Sankt Knuds Vej 11,
basement left, DK-1903 Frederiksberg, Denmark.
Tel.: +45 35 43 60 40, Fax: +45 35 43 87 57. e-mail:
eirdk@hotmail.com.

Mexico City: EIR, Sor Juana Inés de la Cruz 242-2
Col. Agricultura C.P. 11360
Delegación M. Hidalgo, México D.F.
Tel. (5525) 5318-2301
eirmexico@gmail.com

Canada Post Publication Sales Agreement
#40683579

Postmaster: Send all address changes to *EIR*, P.O.
Box 17390, Washington, D.C. 20041-0390.

Signed articles in *EIR* represent the views of the
authors, and not necessarily those of the Editorial
Board.

Bertrand Russell Was Wrong; Human Creativity Can Overcome This Crisis!

Editorial

Bertrand Russell Was Wrong; Human Creativity Can Overcome This Crisis!

Jan 21—You know,— those of you who have not become personally totally demoralized,— you know that this country and much of the world are in an existential crisis. This is far worse than 2008, and far worse than 1929. In the United States, you would have to go back to the pre-Civil War period, or to the time before our Revolutionary War, to find such a level of threat to our country. Nations including our own could effectively cease to exist before this cruel winter ends.

This is a season of death here. Cut off from hope, cut off from a useful existence, cut off from everything, many of our citizens are simply going out to kill themselves, whether with heroin or firearms.

In the trans-Atlantic area, we have a disaster which has apparently little or no future for mankind. However, in terms of Russia and China, we do have something that could be the answer to the problem. You have to understand that the history of mankind in recent times, has been that Asia has been a different region from the trans-Atlantic area. And it's the trans-Atlantic area, as centered in the British Empire, which is the primary source of all the evil that's hitting now.

The key to understanding this, is the history of the British Empire. The British Empire is the source of evil, whereas you have a different possibility available in terms of Russia and China.

For mankind, there is always an available solution to this kind of problem. Where does it lie?

It lies in human creativity, and yes,— you can get there. On certain conditions. In order to get there, you will have to abandon most of the baggage you would like to carry with you. Which is essentially the British Empire, and those parts of the planet which are tied to the British Empire.

Like the current financial system. This financial system is a fake. It's the source of the destruction. You have to get rid of the financial system,— and that is the key to the solution.

As soon as we do that, the bleeding will stop!

It is Bertrand Russell who created this, and it was Bertrand Russell's influence on the U.S. economy, and related things, which caused this destruction.

This problem goes back to the death of the great genius Gottfried Leibniz at the end of 1716. Leibniz was the key to that entire period of history; his death left a huge gap among our forces. Leibniz was the inspirer of the American Revolution, along with much else. Later, decades after Leibniz's death, it was the genius Alexander Hamilton who came forward to pick up Leibniz's role and effectively found the U.S.A. Only Hamilton's economic principles make sense: forget everything else!

Our crisis today is far worse than what Franklin Roosevelt faced, but the same Hamiltonian principles apply. Those principles can bring about a turnaround and eventual recovery now, as they did then. The problem is that so many of our citizens have become too stupid to grasp them. The stupidity which is manifest in submission to Wall Street, and even more particularly to the FBI system which substantially took power in the United States beginning in 1944, even before Franklin Roosevelt's death. It was the introduction of the FBI system which has caused the destruction of the economy of the United States.

Our citizens' minds have fallen prey to the evil influence of London's Lord Bertrand Russell (1872-1970), whom Lyndon LaRouche has called "the most evil man of the Twentieth Century." Russell devoted his life to making men stupid so that they might be easily controlled,— or, as now, killed. His method was to insist on mathematical thinking, which has long been the leading form of abject stupidity worldwide. Beginning in 1900, he succeeded, and progressively destroyed the Twentieth and Twenty-first Centuries. For most of you, this is what you "learned" in school. If you have children, this is all they are so-called "learning," and in a more wretchedly stupid form. This is the stupidity which Albert Einstein, like Lyndon LaRouche, never accepted, and spent most of his life fighting.

Now let's finally get rid of this nonsense. Your life, and a lot more besides, depends on it.

EIR Contents

www.larouchepub.com Volume 43, Number 5, January 29, 2016

Cover This Week

"Baby at Play"
by Thomas
Eakins, 1876

I. Russell's Culture of Death

The Facts of the British Genocide Against the U.S.A.

The following is an edited transcript of excerpts from LaRouche PAC Weekly Webcast of Jan. 22.

Matthew Ogden: Good Evening! It's Jan. 22, 2016. My name is Matthew Ogden, and you're joining us here for our weekly Friday evening LaRouche PAC webcast, here on larouchepac.com.

What we're going to begin with tonight is the astounding evidence of a complete economic disintegration in the United States, among the formerly-productive generation and workforce layers, which has now begun experiencing an astounding surge of death rates over the course of both the Bush and Obama Presidencies, literally since the repeal of Glass-Steagall in 1999. The economic disintegration that we're now seeing taking place in Wall Street and elsewhere is merely just the tip of the iceberg of a complete meltdown of this civilization that we're experiencing now.

The economic blow-out is much, much more than merely the wiping out of what were really just fraudulent stock values to begin with. What this is really about, is *the surging death rates* among the American people themselves. This is very well demonstrated, for example, in the case study of what's happening in Flint, Michigan, right now; which is a direct consequence of the "vulture funds" and the policies of Wall Street, and also the refusal by the Obama administration to intervene on behalf of the people of Michigan two years ago during the Detroit bankruptcy situation.

But this is dwarfed, in comparison when you look at the just recently released study, which I think is emblematic of the dark age that the American people are now experiencing, that was just published in the *New York Times* January 19. Now, on this website, we've covered the study that was published about two months ago, in the beginning of November, by two Princeton economists, including one Nobel Laureate, a study which shocked the American people, wherein they documented that there was an increased mortality among the white non-Hispanic population between the ages of 45 and 54,—really the people who should be in the prime of their productive life and the former industrial middle class.

This is what took place over the course of the Bush and Obama administrations, and had brought about the unnecessary deaths, in *their* terms, of one half of a million Americans—500,000 Americans—who are dead now, who should not be.

It's Really Much Broader

However, that turns out to just be a very narrow slice of the reality of what is actually going on. Following up on that study by these two Princeton economists, the *New York Times* did their own study in which they analyzed nearly 60 million death certificates that were collected by the Centers for Disease Control and Prevention between 1990 and 2014. It found that this death rate among the middle-aged white American population, between the ages of 45 and 54, was actually dwarfed by an even worse condition of death rates for adults of a younger age group. This study in the *New York Times* was published on Wednesday, under a major graphic on the front page, which shows how America's drug overdose epidemic spread.

What the *New York Times* found is that the major increase in the death rates among this entire layer of the American population was driven by *drug overdoses and suicides*. Some of the statistics on this are absolutely astounding. But, before I get to that, let me just show a graphic which is a screen shot from the *New York Times* website, which shows, year-upon-year, from 2003 until 2014, how these drug overdose deaths

FIGURE 1
Death Rates for Drug Poisoning 2002

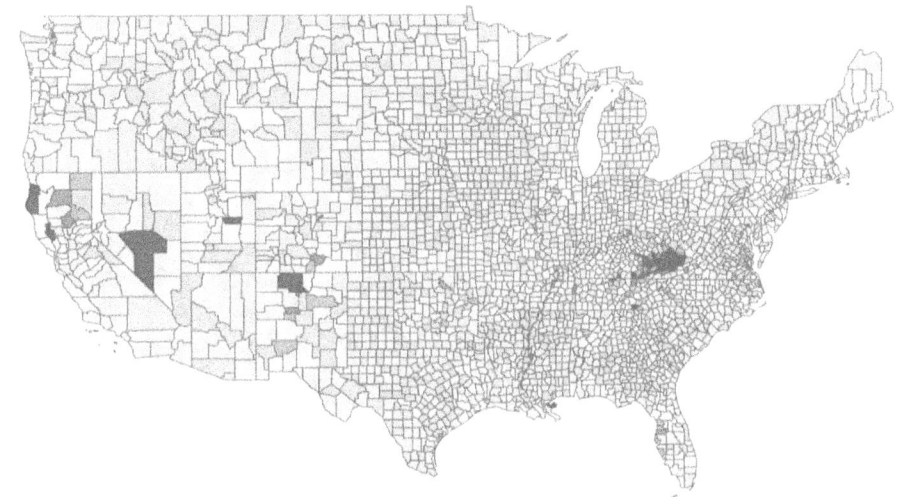

CDC/NCHS, National Vital Statistics System

The two maps indicate primarily deaths from heroin and prescription drug overdoses. Blue represents 0-4 deaths per 100,000 population; red is 20-24 deaths per 100,000.

FIGURE 2
Death Rates for Drug Poisoning 2014

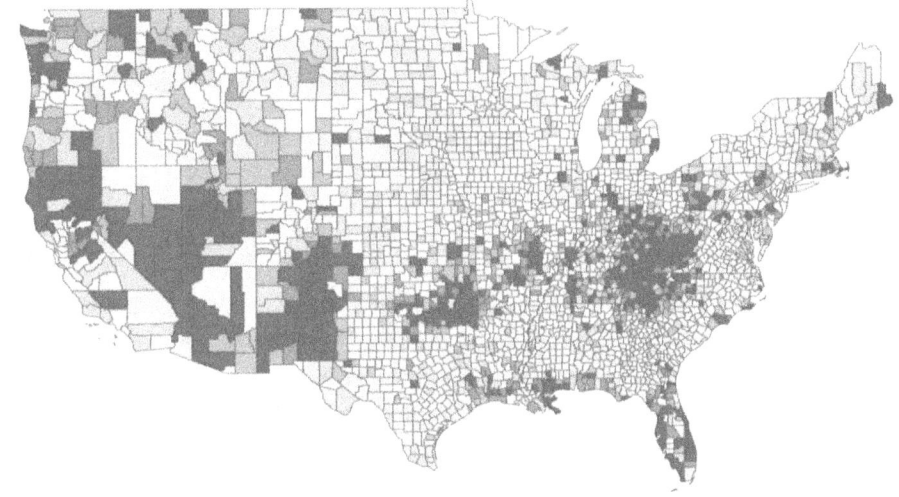

CDC/NCHS, National Vital Statistics System

Comparison of the maps for 2002 and 2014 shows the rapid spread of this epidemic.

experienced an increase in these drug overdose deaths, with a huge concentration of counties that are now seeing over 20 deaths per 100,000.

Let me show the next slide, here [Figure 1]. This slide is a close-up of data from the CDC, which shows, in 2002, where the concentrations of these overdoses were happening. You can see the biggest concentration was in Appalachia, in West Virginia and in surrounding areas of Southwest Virginia, Tennessee, Kentucky. This is the former coal mining area. You also see a concentration in the Southwest, in Nevada, in New Mexico.

Take a look at the next slide [Figure 2]. This is 2014. Not only have those areas in Appalachia and in the Southwest metastasized and spread, but now you see this sweeping all the way across the country. There's not one region which is not affected by this epidemic.

Take a look at the next slide, here [Figures 1 and 2]. This is a comparison between 2002, the beginning of the Bush administration, and 2014. This is the last year that we have data available, and one can only imagine what the data is for 2015, and going into 2016.

The demographic breakdown of this is absolutely astounding. Since 1999, the drug-related death rates among the

have spread to take over the entire United States. What this is showing, is a county-by-county breakdown of heroin overdoses and also prescription drug overdoses, per 100,000 people. You can see that the blue color is 0-4 deaths per 100,000. And then the red, all the way up the spectrum, is 20-24 deaths per 100,000. You can see that *almost every single county* in the United States has

white American population within the 25-34 age group—both among men and women—have increased by 500%! This is broken down according to drug overdoses, where in 1999 you had 6 per every 100,000 people died of a drug overdose, and in 2014 it was 30 of every 100,000 people—a 500% increase, over 15 years. During that same period, suicides among that age group went up from 15 per 100,000, to almost 20 per 100,000. If we go up to the next age bracket, between the ages of 35 and 44, you can see that drug overdoses increases increased from 9 per 100,000, to 30 per 100,000. That is a 300% increase. And, between the ages of 45 and 54—this was the age group that the two Princeton economists studied in their published work—drug overdoses increased from 6.7 to 30 per 100,000, which is a 400% increase. And suicides increased from 16 to 26 per 100,000.

Now, the *New York Times* study, which was published on Tuesday, and then followed up with a major front-page article that was published on Wednesday, I think, rightly, points out that this is a shock to people who have looked at this. It quotes Dr. Wilson Compton, the Deputy Director of the National Institute on Drug Abuse, who said, "This is absolutely startling. These are tremendous increases." And, what's absolutely shocking about this, is that this has caused the overall death rate of this layer of the American population to *increase* over this time, offsetting what should have been a *decrease* in the death rates because of increases and improvements in medical technology; the treatment and prevention of heart disease, of cancer; and so forth. Despite the fact that there were increases in medical technology and a decrease of death rate from these so-called "natural" causes, the overall death rate was increasing, because of drug overdoses, suicide, alcoholism, and related forms of death.

Who is "Too Big to Fail?"

What we're seeing here is an epidemic of hopelessness, and that this is not a purely drug-related question; this is an economic question. And this is reflective of a complete breakdown of the economic productivity of the American people, and a surge in complete lack of a sense of mission, a sense of future; and hopelessness among this layer of the American people.

This is the reality of the situation that we have now found ourselves in after 14-15 years of first a Bush/Cheney administration, and then an Obama administration. And, literally, if you take this period of time, between 1999-2000 and now 2014-2015, this is the period since the repeal of Glass-Steagall, and the policies of both the Bush and Obama administrations, to sacrifice the American people on the altar of the bail-outs of

creative commons/Dow Jones Events
Lanny Breuer, Assistant Attorney General for the Criminal Division of the Department of Justice under Obama: "If we were to prosecute these banks, it would threaten the integrity of the entire trans-Atlantic financial system."

these Wall Street banks. And that's a very relevant point because not only are we seeing a spread of heroin usage, opioid usage, on the level of just the general population, which crosses all sociological barriers. It's no longer concentrated just to inner cities, or just to even rural poor whites, but this is crossing over to every single level, every single income bracket, across the entire country. Rural Appalachia, suburban areas, families whose incomes are higher than $50,000 a year, inner cities, everywhere, every corner of the United States.

Take a look at the policies of the Obama administration, for example, who have found that every single one of the major Wall Street banks has been up to their elbows in drug-money laundering: Wachovia, Citibank, HSBC. Each one of these has been found guilty of dealing with drug cartels in Mexico, South America, elsewhere, and it's been thoroughly documented, such as in a Senate report that was published two years ago, by the Senate Permanent Investigation Subcommittee, chaired by Sen. Carl Levin, which documented the case of the drug-money laundering that was committed by HSBC.

What has been the official position of the Obama administration, and of the Obama Justice Department? Not one of these banks will be prosecuted. Why? They're "too big to fail." As Lanny Breuer, who was Assistant Attorney General for the Criminal Division in the Obama administration Justice Department, stated, "If we were to prosecute these banks, it would threaten the integrity of the entire trans-Atlantic financial system." Which I think proves, beyond a shadow of a doubt, that this entire financial system is *founded* on criminality and fraud.

The blood is on the hands of the people (the Bush and Obama administrations) who have failed to address the fact that there's been an official policy to say Wall Street banks will be protected while the American population and the productive powers of that population are thrown on the junk heap.

We're looking at a situation now which is far worse than 2008, as Mr. LaRouche has stressed, and in many ways, is far worse than 1929-32. The question is, what policy must be implemented in order to reverse this dark age, and reverse this trajectory in the death rates among the American people, which is reaching the point of unprecedented levels? The policy of Glass-Steagall, the policy of breaking up these Wall Street banks has to be seen from the standpoint of not just a financial reform policy; but that this is the criminal element in the United States, and this is the cause of the increase in the death rates among our fellow American people.

Then again, if we turn around and say, among these young people, for example, who have experienced a 500% increase in the rates of drug overdoses and suicides in just the past 14 years: What can be done to give these young people a sense of the a future? The CCC of Franklin Roosevelt is a very necessary precedent; the work-relief programs of the first 100 days is a very necessary precedent. This is the population which must be employed and put to work through Federal employment projects to get the American people back into a future-oriented mission-orientation. However, as Mr. LaRouche said earlier today, we have reached a point where we are so far gone, that it's not going to just be through a partial replication of policies that have come before that we can save this system. The entire system must be junked, and we have to look to the policies that are now taking place in places such as China and allied countries among the BRICS, as the example for what must be done in the United States. I think this is very clearly documented in *The United States Joins the New*

Ogden: *"The entire system must be junked."*

Silk Road special report that's just been published by the La-Rouche Political Action Committee; and these are the policies which we've laid out in very clear terms...

So, I'd like to introduce Jeff Steinberg to elaborate a little bit more on what Mr. LaRouche's points were in response to this, during our discussion earlier today.

Where Did This Come From?

Jeffrey Steinberg: Thanks, Matt. Mr. LaRouche has been persistently making the point that you've got to remove President Obama from office if you're going to even have a chance to begin addressing the problems that have now been presented in very stark kind of snapshot terms by these three *New York Times* studies. Now, I think it's important to remember that the phony statistics that are repeated like a daily mantra by the Obama administration and most of the mainstream media, that the U.S. economy is recovering, that unemployment is now down to 5%, is a very conscious fraud. Remember that there are now more than 94 million people who are of working age, who are not in school, who are not in military service, who are not in jail, and who are not in various medical institutions; 94 million people between the ages of 18 and 65, who are not counted as part of the labor force because they are either chronically unemployed, or have not yet ever been able to find a job. So that 94 million people represents almost one quarter of the American population, who have been consciously thrown on the scrap heap; and that's not to even take into account the children of those people who've been written out of the equation, or the senior citizens who are living in the kinds of poverty conditions that Franklin Roosevelt insisted would never happen again.

Now, Mr. LaRouche's point is very clear: This is not something that was simply conjured up by George W. Bush or Dick Cheney or Barack Obama. This is a policy that has come down from the British. In 1979, *Executive Intelligence Review* published the first of what are now five updated editions of the book *Dope, Inc.*; in which we detailed and documented that the British were conducting an opium war against the United States with the idea of destroying the United States in terms of the principles on which the republic was founded

So, if you take what Matt just presented—these three *New York Times* reports, which merely provide a snapshot of where things stand now; you've got to next ask the question, "How did we get here?" There's no dispute that for a growing and sizeable portion of the American population, the whole idea of the American dream has been ripped away and torn apart. As Mr. LaRouche was emphasizing in our discussions today, the state of the labor force, particularly the younger elements of the population, was better in 1933 when Roosevelt came into office and launched his First 100 Days program than the population is today. Young people are addicted to video games; in many instances, violent video games that have produced things like the youth killers in Paducah, Kentucky, in Littleton, Colorado, the many instances that go unreported in the national media today, because they're just so commonplace.

So, you've got to ask yourself, how did this come about? Where did this phenomenon come from? And again, Mr. LaRouche has emphasized that if you don't understand the hatred by the British Empire for what the United States represented, as a revolutionary republican culture in its first generation, then you can't understand what happened during the course of the Twentieth Century, and now into the beginning of the Twenty-first Century. You can't appreciate what has been done to the United States, unless you go back and look at this factor of the British assault, the British hatred. What we, when we wrote *Dope, Inc.*, called the "British opium war" against the United States. Remember, in the middle of the 19th Century, the British launched wars in order to impose opium addiction and destroy the population of China, as part of a looting operation that took the form of two Opium Wars and a massive enforced opium addiction on China. We're seeing the same thing happening here in the United States today; and it's not a new story.

I want to review with you, over the next few moments, some of the *statements of intent* that have been issued by prominent voices of the British Empire. And at the end of that, I want you to ask yourself a question. Is there any longer any confusion in your mind in terms of what Mr. LaRouche talks about when he discusses the British Empire as the root cause of the problem?

Obama and Bertrand Russell

Now, we can just start, of course, with the case of Barack Obama. Barack Obama was essentially picked up and created as a political entity by British networks. One of the most prominent figures in the entire career development of Barack Obama, was George Soros; who is not only a British agent—and fully documented and certified as such—but Soros has been the driving force, the source of financing for several decades for the entire movement to legalize all illegal drugs in the United States. If you think it was merely a matter of medical use of marijuana, I can tell you from personal experience, having attended conferences of Soros' Drug Policy Foundation going back 20 years ago; where in private discussions behind closed doors, Soros openly said—and his representatives openly said—that the objective was the legalization of all drugs. Crack cocaine, heroin, you name it. So, now we're seeing the consequences and fruits of that. When Obama was elected President of the United States, back in 2008, with George Soros' money a prominent feature of that, the message radiated out to all the drug-producing countries of the world, that it was an open door to start flooding the United States with even larger amounts of illegal drugs; because the efforts at stopping it will be minimal and eventually inconsequential. So, it's not just a matter that people, out of despair, out of desperation, have turned to illegal drugs; those drugs are now available in vast quantities and at greatly reduced prices in every county in the United States.

So the figures, the 47,000 people who died of drug overdoses in the United States in 2014 alone, is merely a statistical marker for what is actually going on. But again, I want to take up the larger question: *What was the intent?* What were the statements of intent? What was the vision of a future United States, represented by some of the leading powerful voices of the British Empire? We've quoted previously from Lord Bertrand Russell, but it's always useful to recall his own words about what his view and what his intentions were towards the United States and towards the world as a whole. In 1951, Russell wrote in his book, *The Impact of Science on Society* about the targeting of young people for menticide, for destruction. He wrote:

Physiology and psychology afford fields for sci-

EIRNS/Stuart Lewis

George Soros and his Drug Policy Foundation (now the Drug Policy Alliance) provided the money and the prestige to promote the legalization of all drugs, to advance the program of Bertrand Russell and his collaborators. Clockwise from top left: Soros, Russell, Aldous Huxley, and Julian Huxley.

when it is taken up by scientists under scientific dictatorship. The social psychologists of the future will have a number of classes of school children; on whom they will try different methods of producing an unshakeable conviction that snow is black. Various results will soon be arrived at. First, that the influence of home is obstructive. Secondly, that not much can be done unless indoctrination begins before the age of ten. Third, that verses set to music and repeatedly intoned are very effective. Fourth, that the opinion that snow is white must be held to show a morbid taste for eccentricity.

But I anticipate. It is for future scientists to make these maxims precise, and to discover exactly how much it costs per head, to make children believe that snow is black; and how much less it would cost to make them believe it is dark gray.

entific technique which still await development. Two great men—Pavlov and Freud—have laid the foundation. I do not accept the view that they are in any essential conflict, but what structure will be built on their foundations is still in doubt. I think the subject which will be of most importance politically, is mass psychology; its importance has been enormously increased by the growth of modern methods of propaganda. Of these, the most influential is what is called education; religion plays a part, though a diminishing one. The press, the cinema, and the radio play an increasing part. It may be hoped that in time, anybody will be able to persuade anybody of anything if he can catch the patient young, and is provided by the state with money and equipment. The subject will make great strides

And then he says: "Although this science will be diligently studied, it will be rigidly confined to the governing class. The populace will not be allowed to know how its convictions were generated. When the technique has been perfected, every government that has been in charge of education for a generation, will be able to control its subjects securely, without the need of armies or policemen."

There are other, even earlier quotes from Russell, showing the same intent. He wrote in 1931 in *The Scientific Outlook*, where he had a chapter devoted to education in a scientific society. He said,

> The scientific rulers will provide one kind of education for ordinary men and women, and another for those who are to become holders of scientific power. Ordinary men and women will be expected to be docile, industrious, punctual, thoughtless, and contented. Of these qualities, probably contentment will be considered the most important. In order to produce it, all the remedies of psychoanalysis, behaviorism, and biochemistry will be brought into play. All the boys and girls will learn from an early age to be what is called 'cooperative'; i.e., to do exactly what everybody is doing. Initiative will be discouraged in these children; insubordination without punishment will be scientifically trained out of them.

The Drugging of America

In other words, a conscious attempt to guarantee that future generations will have no capacity for creative discovery. Now, Russell and many of his collaborators, including the brothers Aldous and Julian Huxley, understood that it was going to be vital to spread this ideology and this spreading of drugs into society; and that the opium war against the United States, was an absolutely indispensable part of the assault against the cognitive powers of the population, particularly focused on young people. Aldous Huxley came to the United States in the 1920s; and not surprisingly, he immediately found his way to Hollywood, where he became part of a circle of British ideologues who were dominant behind the scenes in the mass culture industry in Hollywood. There was a whole grouping from the 1920s on in Hollywood that was known as the "British set." It included people like Aldous Huxley and Christopher Isherwood, and Igor Stravinsky, who was part of the assault on music that was a core feature of this Twentieth Century attack. Huxley was part of the MK-Ultra programs that devel-

Harvard psychology professor Timothy Leary, one of Aldous Huxley's closest collaborators: "We had run up against the Judeo-Christian commitment to one God, one religion, one reality that has cursed Europe for centuries, and America since our founding days."

oped the means by which to spread various kinds of psychotropic and other kinds of drugs into the population. And Aldous Huxley, in an address in 1961, to a conference sponsored by the U.S. government's Voice of America, at the California state medical school in San Francisco, was very blunt. This was not fiction; this was his statement of intent for what future generations in this country would be experiencing and would be put through. He said:

> There will be in the next generation or so, a pharmacological method of making people love their servitude and producing dictatorship without tears, so to speak. Producing a kind of painless concentration camp for entire societies; so that people will, in fact, have their liberties taken away from them, but will rather enjoy it, because they will distracted from any desire to rebel, by propaganda, or brainwashing, or brainwashing enhanced by pharmacological methods. And this seems to be the final revolution.

Now, Huxley was part of the experimentation in psychedelic drugs that was partly U.S.- and British-government sponsored and financed from the 1950s onward. And one of Huxley's closest collaborators was a Harvard professor of psychology, named Timothy Leary; who became one of the leading propagandists for the use of psychotropic drugs. Leary wrote a personal account of his involvement in this drug counterculture project; and at one point, reflected on conversations that he had personally had with Aldous Huxley. He said that he recalled Huxley telling him the following: "These brain drugs, mass produced in laboratories, will bring about vast changes in society. This will happen without you or without me. All we can do is spread the word. The obstacle to this revolution, Timmy, is the Bible." Leary then provided his own comment: "We had run up against the Judeo-Christian commitment to one God, one religion, one reality that has cursed Europe for centuries, and America since our founding days. Drugs that open the mind to multiple realities inevitably lead to a polytheistic view of the universe. We sensed that the time for a new humanist religion based on intelligence, good-natured pluralism, and scientific paganism had arrived."

So, this just gives you a brief flavor for what we're looking at. I mentioned Aldous Huxley and quoted from him just now; his brother Julian, who was the founding director of UNESCO back in 1946, made it very clear that even though Hitler had been defeated, and the racial science policies, and the eugenics policies at the core of the Nazi movement had been discredited, that these were British ideas that would be brought once again to the fore. Julian Huxley, in his opening address at the launching of UNESCO in 1946 declared, "Even though it is quite true that any radical eugenic policy will be for many years politically and psychologically impossible, it will be important for UNESCO to see that the eugenic problem is examined with the greatest care; and that the public mind is informed of the issues at stake. So that much that is now unthinkable may at least become thinkable."

Mass Brainwashing

Now, as one element of the MK-Ultra drug experimental programs of the 1950s, which was principally a British program, there were extensive studies on how to use forms of mass psychology to create the conditions where people would willfully submit to the kinds of menticide and despair that were basically planned by the British. William Sargant, a Tavistock Institute psychiatrist who served in the British military at a certain point, was one of the critical players who was brought over from Britain to the United States as part of MK-Ultra. In 1957 he wrote a book, *Battle for the Mind*, in which he discussed certain core principles about how to conduct the mass brainwashing of the American people. And bear in mind that he wrote this book six years before the assassination of John F. Kennedy; but think about the Kennedy assassination, think about the Martin Luther King assassination, the Robert Kennedy assassination, the Vietnam War, the riots that plagued the United States in the 1960s, and the cultural paradigm shift that was effected. And let's see what William Sargant said about that in 1957; he wrote:

Various types of belief can be implanted in many people after brain function has been sufficiently disturbed by accidentally or deliberately induced fear, anger, or excitement. Of the results caused by such disturbances, the common one is temporarily impaired judgement and heightened suggestibility. Its various group manifestations were sometimes classed under the heading of 'herd instinct' and appear most spectacularly in war-time, in severe epidemics, and in all similar periods of common danger, which increase anxiety and also individual and mass suggestibility.

So, you've got this continuing pursuit of means of conducting mass psychological assaults against an entire population. You had the waves of assassinations and wars and riots that caught the United States throughout the 1960s. What was the outcome of that? You had the advent of the mass rock/drug/sex counterculture; because young people, suddenly for the first time, felt that the world was completely chaotic, was collapsing. And that the concept of a viable future was no longer quite so certain. You also had the advent and the cumulative effects of more than a century by this point, of a conscious assault against the principle of renaissance that had last been seen in the great musical compositions of the middle towards the end of the 19th Century; when you had Beethoven, Schubert, Schumann, Brahms.

And suddenly, at the beginning of the 20th Century, all of the great advancements, all of those renaissance breakthroughs were shut off; and instead, you were presented with a culture of ugliness, of banality, and of perversion. Again, this was not something that just happened as the result of bad luck. One of the major networks that was brought into the United States under British Fabian sponsorship to spread this concept of cultural pessimism and irrationalism, was an organization known as the Frankfurt School, established in Germany in 1922 and which was part of a revolutionary movement that concluded that during times of war, during times of great crisis, the working class populations tended to become extremely patriotic. And the Frankfurt School revolutionary movements, associated also with people like Georg Lukacs, had concluded that the real revolution had to take the form of an assault against the fundamental tenets of modern western European culture—which was already degenerate, and therefore opened up an enormous opportunity.

One of the leaders of the Frankfurt School, Theodor

Continuators of Russell's program. Clockwise from top left: Tavistock Institute psychiatrist William Sargant, Theodor Adorno of the Frankfurt School, modernist composer Igor Stravinsky, and atonal composer Arnold Schoenberg. In a book about Schoenberg and Stravinsky, Adorno wrote, "Modern music sees absolute oblivion as its goal."

Man Ray   George Grantham Bain Collection, U.S. Library of Congress

Adorno, came to the United States in the mid-1930s. He went to work at Princeton University in a Rockefeller-funded program called the Radio Research Project; that aimed to study how populations could be manipulated by the new advent of mass communications technology—movies, radio, the early emergence of television. Adorno had a background and training in music; in fact, he was a student of Schoenberg, who was one of the original composers to introduce atonal music, which was a total assault on Classical composition. Adorno, as a conscious part of this British assault against American

and generally speaking Western culture, wrote a book in 1948 addressing the question of modern music. It was called *The Philosophy of Modern Music*, and the basic theme of the book, which was a series of essays dealing with Schoenberg and Stravinsky, was that modern music, completely in contrast to great Classical music, was intended not to uplift people and to make a direct appeal to their human creativity, to their soul; but was to bring them down and to actually destroy their capacity to think. Adorno was very explicit in the idea that modern music intended to create forms of mental illness, or to tap into mental illnesses and bring them to the surface.

A Century-Long Assault

This is from Adorno's 1948 book, *The Philosophy of Modern Music:* "What radical music perceives is the untransfigured suffering, the seismographic registration of traumatic shock, becomes at the same time the technical structure of music. It forbids continuity and development." (Which is obviously the key to music.) "Musical language is polarized according to its extremes towards gestures of shock, resembling bodily convulsions on the one hand and on the other, towards a crystalline standstill of a human being whom anxiety causes to stop in her tracks. Modern music sees absolute oblivion as its goal; it is a surviving message of despair from the shipwrecked." He continues: "It is not that schizophrenia is directly expressed therein; but the music imprints upon itself an attitude similar to that of the mentally ill. The individual brings about his own disintegration. He imagines the fulfillment of the promise through magic, but nonetheless, within the realm of immediate actuality. Its concern is to dominate schizophrenic traits through an aesthetic consciousness. In so doing, it would hope to vindicate insanity as true Hell."

Now, Adorno goes on to catalogue various forms of mental disease that can be instigated and accentuated by exposure to modern music; by which he meant not only the atonality of Schoenberg and Stravinsky, but the background noise, the Muzak, the pop-40 kind of music that was then becoming a major feature of American culture as it began a long steady process of degeneration. He asked: What would be the consequences of repeated exposure to these kinds of music? Depersonalization, which he describes as the loss of connection to one's own body. Hebephrenia, which he defines as indifference of the sick individual towards the external. Catatonia; disassociation of time. And ultimately, universal necrophilia is the highest perversity of style.

Obviously, in this brief time, I've just scratched the surface. And I've only touched on a few of the leading criminals of the British Empire, who have focused their attention on the destruction of the underlying culture of the United States—the menticide, targeting successive generations of young people. And we have the report that Matt began this broadcast with, dealing with the fact that we're there; we've reached the point where millions, perhaps tens of millions of Americans have been thrown onto an economic and cultural scrap heap. Where they have no opportunity, no sense of the future; where despair is manifesting in its most extreme form in drug addiction, heroin overdoses, suicides. Those are the most shocking, extreme forms; but for every case where that has happened, how many millions of others, how many people do you know personally, who are chronically out of work; who've developed a sense of absolute despair about the world, about their own future, about future generations, which is always the hallmark of a growing society.

So, step back and think about the fact that there has been a more than 100-year conscious cultural assault against the United States. Yes, there have been dramatic developments; there have been assassinations of presidents. We had the spectre of the Bush/Cheney administration launching a string of absolutely needless wars to impose a police state structure on the United States. We've had Obama opening the floodgates for this opium war assault, which is in its most advanced stages right now. But go back; think about where this comes from. And only from that standpoint can we begin to have a serious discussion about remedies.

Cannibalization of the American People

Ogden: Thank you, Jeff. Now, just to say, this astounding rise in death rates that has been documented thoroughly in these *New York Times* studies, is a direct consequence of the ideology that Jeff just very thoroughly documented; which has come to dominate much of the Twentieth Century, and is now literally leading to the cannibalization of the American people by a system which is based axiomatically on that ideology. This is hitting hardest among the youth generation; it's literally destroying the future of the United States. It's that 25-34 year old generation which has experienced among the white demographic, a 500% increase in death rates from drug overdoes over these past 15 years. I think, correctly, as the *New York Times* article states, "The rising death rates for these young white adults, aged 25-34, make them the first generation since the Vietnam War years of the mid-1960s, to experience death rates in early adulthood than the generation that preceded it." That's a dark age.

The study also points out that there's a very clear delineation among the less-educated layers of the population; it says that these death rates that rose among that age group, rose faster by any measure for the less educated. A 23% increase in death rates among those without a high school degree; compared to only 4% for those with a college degree. So, you can see, it's the most vulnerable, it's literally the forgotten man which is dying *en masse*. The astounding statistic is the number of U.S. drug overdose deaths reached a new high in the year 2014, which is the last year with complete records. 47,055 people died in drug overdose deaths during the year 2015; which averages out to an average of 125 people every single day.

So, I think what's clear is, in combination with the evidence that's presented in this study, and what Jeff just went through in documenting this British imperialistic ideology which has come to dominate much of the 20th Century since the rise of Bertrand Russell; is that there's no solution to this without having a completely new paradigm. Where this system, which is based axiomatically on anti-human principles, must be replaced by a completely new paradigm; a renaissance. And as I stated earlier in this broadcast, what Mr. LaRouche emphasized is that the solution to this dark age that is being experienced by the American people must be seen as not something that can just merely be solved by some sort of reforms of the system. But that you have to take the impulse that's coming from China and related countries, who are actively pursuing a policy of economic development and a scientific and cultural renaissance; and use that to create as the foundation for an entirely new paradigm to replace this failed paradigm in the trans-Atlantic system.

THE ESSENTIAL TRUTH OF THE TWENTIETH CENTURY

How Bertrand Russell Made Us Stupid, Fearful, and Evil

by Paul Glumaz

Jan 23—Today as I look around, it is clear to me that the United States is dying—and so are the nations of Europe. Sixty-six years elapsed from the Wright brothers' first flight in 1903 to the Moon landing. Today, forty-seven years after the Moon landing, an increasing number of people believe that the Moon landing was a staged hoax. Those in our society today who have leisure, are more interested in life-style issues, entertainment, and exploring their "inner space," than they are about caring for future generations, or even for their own children.

The financial system of North America and Europe is collapsing. It is no longer really a financial system, but a system of gambling. Drug addiction and suicides are dramatically escalating, along with, in the case of the United States, mass murders by random individuals. Perhaps as much as half the population of Europe and North America are either taking some variety of mood-altering prescription drugs or smoking pot, while tens of millions are drowning in drugs or alcohol in order to be able to "cope."

What happened to us? Are we that stupid? Are we that uncaring? Are we that depraved? Are we that depressed? Are we that evil that we would launch a nuclear war against our "enemies," Russia and China, if they don't agree to become like us? Emphatically,—yes, we are all of those things. What happened?

Oligarch Bertrand Russell in 1907. Publication of Principia Mathematica, *written jointly with Alfred North Whitehead, began in 1910. He inherited the family earldom in 1931.*

What happened, is that over the course of the Twentieth Century, we came under the influence, primarily, of one man, Bertrand Russell. That single individual has done more by far to shape how we think, what we believe, and the world we are living in, than any individual in modern history. What follows is an explanation of how he accomplished that.

How He Made Us Stupid

As elaborated in Russell's work with Alfred North Whitehead, *Principia Mathematica,* which began to appear in 1910, Bertrand Russell attempted to eliminate reality from mathematics (and then from science),—replacing reality with Aristotelean logic.

He began with Arithmetic. Bertrand Russell popularized the false claim—the quackery—that Arithmetic could be deduced from Logic. From there, Russell claimed that all mathematics could be deduced from Arithmetic,—and therefore from Logic. No real scientist could ever believe in either of these hoaxes of Russell's, but all the resources of the British Empire were used to assert their inevitability. For those who needed a formal refutation of this nonsense, the Austrian mathematician Kurt Gödel furnished a formal proof of Russell's fraud in 1931, which even Russell could not contest.

Gödel proved conclusively that even simple Arithmetic, let alone the rest of Mathematics, could never be deduced from Logic. Unable to reply to Gödel, an enraged Russell persecuted him savagely for the rest of his life.

Bertrand Russell's consumer fraud in claiming that he had reduced Arithmetic to mere logic, is then used to try to convince people that our knowledge of the universe is derived from the operations of logic on our sensory observations of the world. Anyone familiar with computers can tell you that no matter how complex the computer logic is, it cannot create anything beyond the logic in its program. It cannot make a discovery. It cannot think. This is true with all logic. Discovering things cannot occur in a logical system. The axioms of the system deductively predetermine the outcome. Human thinking is not logical, never has been, and never will be. The only human beings who are logical are the ones who have been taught to be logical. Logic is not natural to human beings. It is not how we make discoveries, nor is it how we really know anything.

In Russell's *Principles of Mathematics* (1903) he writes: "The fact that all Mathematics is Symbolic Logic is one of the greatest discoveries of our age; and when this fact has been established, the remainder of the principles of mathematics consists in the analysis of Symbolic Logic itself." *Principles of Mathematics.* 1903. See Chap. I: Definition of Pure Mathematics, p. 5. *Pure fraud!* A long-exploded hoax.

How many people reading this have been taught to believe that reasoning is logic, and that to learn how to think, you need to learn logic? The confusion of logic with reason and reason with logic is probably the greatest cause of the inability of our population to have confidence in the power of their own minds to discover and solve problems. From a political standpoint it is probably the greatest cause of why most people abandon their responsibility to think, or cannot challenge the obvious false axioms they are told to think in, because they believe that rational human thinking only occurs as logic.

It is worse than that. All things that are not logical are relegated to the realm of the "not scientific." All issues involving creativity in the universe, whether by man or the universe as a whole, are not scientific. All issues involving intention in the universe, are outside of logic, and are not scientific. All issues involving principles that are metaphysical, that is directing the physical, are not scientific. All matters involving a direct relationship of the macrocosm, or the whole, to the microcosm, the part, cannot be logically explained and

$$*54\cdot43. \quad \vdash :. \alpha, \beta \epsilon 1 . \supset : \alpha \cap \beta = \Lambda . \equiv . \alpha \cup \beta \epsilon 2$$

Dem.

$$\vdash . *54\cdot26 . \supset \vdash :. \alpha = \iota'x . \beta = \iota'y . \supset : \alpha \cup \beta \epsilon 2 . \equiv . x \neq y .$$
$$[*51\cdot231] \qquad\qquad\qquad\qquad \equiv . \iota'x \cap \iota'y = \Lambda .$$
$$[*13\cdot12] \qquad\qquad\qquad\qquad \equiv . \alpha \cap \beta = \Lambda \qquad (1)$$
$$\vdash . (1) . *11\cdot11\cdot35 . \supset$$
$$\vdash :. (\exists x, y) . \alpha = \iota'x . \beta = \iota'y . \supset : \alpha \cup \beta \epsilon 2 . \equiv . \alpha \cap \beta = \Lambda \qquad (2)$$
$$\vdash . (2) . *11\cdot54 . *52\cdot1 . \supset \vdash . \text{Prop}$$

From this proposition it will follow, when arithmetical addition has been defined, that $1 + 1 = 2$.

From the Principia Mathematica, *a small portion of the proof that $1 + 1 = 2$. Russell created the notation.*

therefore are not scientific.

It is even much worse than that. Since thinking as a human is "not science," then only those trained in logic are qualified to be experts, or to know anything. These properly trained individuals then set the standard of what forms of explanation are allowed in science. This means all discoveries that may be made in science, discoveries that could not have been made by logic, must be explained in a logical form, as if they were derived from that logical form. This not only obscures the method by which the discoveries are made, but on the deepest level creates a situation where the population becomes susceptible to all forms of phantasms, since there is no visible process by which the population can see by example, truthfully, scientifically, the actual process of thought that led to the discovery. This also has both a serious negative effect on the education process, as well as undermining the intellectual confidence of those trying to use their mind in a human way.

So then, what is human reason? Human reason takes the form not of logic, but of a dialogue. There are no pre-existing first principles from which everything is derived, or deduced, while everything outside of that is excluded. Rather, reason involves the dialogue that asks the question of what must be, that we cannot see, if what we know must be *this*, as well as the alternative *that*. Reason, as Einstein has said, involves first and foremost the imagination: imagining that which is outside of what is seen, heard or felt, etc.,—which is as it were the heretofore-hidden ground for these,— which was not previously conceived, and which cannot be known from the senses.

The most notable individual who resisted this reduction of science to mere logic was Albert Einstein. All the other scientists of this period in Europe and the United States did not challenge it as a fundamental point of sup-

Library of Congress

The most notable individual who resisted the pretended reduction of science to logic was Albert Einstein.

posed agreement. Russell retaliated against Einstein's resistance by virtually mugging him: he forced almost every other well-known "scientist" to publicly gang up against Einstein, and then,— when he still refused to submit,— to slander and shun him. As a result, Einstein was essentially banned from scientific dialog for the last twenty years of his life. Einstein said that his "scientific colleagues" considered him a "mountebank,"—i.e., a charlatan or a quack. This is what Russell did to the greatest scientist of the Twentieth Century.

Why Bertrand Russell Made Us Stupid

Bertrand Russell made us stupid because he was the leading intellect of the aristocracy which informed the leading empire of the world, the British Empire. It was the spreading global effect of the industrial revolution that had occurred during the civil war in the United States, and its subsequent consequences, that motivated Bertrand Russell. There was no way of stopping the industrial revolution from conquering the world and ending the rule of aristocracies for all time. Russell's

genius is that he understood that to retard that process, the methods by which discoveries were made had to be attacked. He also recognized that the population that was starting to experience the leisure, and education, that comes with an industrial revolution needed to be drastically dumbed down and made to conform.

In his 1931 book, *The Scientific Outlook,* Russell says, 'Ordinary men and women will be expected to be docile, industrious, punctual, thoughtless, and contented. Of these qualities probably contentment will be considered the most important. In order to produce it, all the researches of psycho-analysis, behaviourism, and biochemistry will be brought into play .... All the boys and girls will learn from an early age to be what is called 'co-operative,' i.e., to do exactly what everybody is doing. Initiative will be discouraged in these children, and insubordination, without being punished, will be scientifically trained out of them.' For the children chosen to be among the scientific ruling class, education was to be quite different. 'Except for the one matter of loyalty to the world State and to their own order,' Russell explained, 'members of the governing class will be encouraged to be adventurous and full of initiative. It will be recognized that it is their business to improve scientific technique, and to keep the manual workers contented by means of continual new amusements'." (Jeffrey Steinberg, "From Cybernetics to Littleton," *EIR*, May 5, 2000)

This is the future that Bertrand Russell envisioned for an aristocracy facing the challenge of both the industrial revolution as well as future scientific and technological revolutions, revolutions which would lead to the "horrid" development of the lower classes to a level of intellect far surpassing that of the aristocracy. In a pre-industrial society it is not necessary to have all the various biochemical, psychoanalytic, pharmaceutical means of control, because the scarcity of means is the control. Russell's idea of science is not industrial and productive development. It is the science of dumbing down the masses and increasing the means "to keep the manual workers contented by means of continual new amusements."

The techniques for dumbing down the population that were proposed by H.G. Wells in his *Open Conspir-*

acy, which Bertrand Russell wholeheartedly supported and endorsed, included the following important key aspects:

• destroying the ability of the language to communicate profound ideas by altering the accepted styles of writing and speech, such as outlawing the subjunctive mood;

• replacing classical music and classical drama with the equivalent of rock-type entertainment; and

• the use of all kinds of drugs and mind-altering substances to enslave people to their senses, so they cannot think.

All this has happened. In this respect we are now living the very future that Bertrand Russell had envisaged for us.

Systems Analysis, the Ultimate Form of Stupidity

Bertrand Russell was the principal leader promoting what is called "systems analysis" as a tool for predicting future outcomes, and of dealing with complex variables to make a scientific analysis of a situation by either breaking something down and analyzing its components, or taking the components and analyzing the whole, based on those components.

This *appears* to be very scientific and very useful. Bertrand Russell advocated that this be used in a universal way to integrate all the sciences, in a system-of-systems manner. This method of analysis, as it was used beyond very limited and specific situations, is the ultimate form of stupidity. It is totally divorced from reality, and seeks to impose on reality the construct created by the systems analyst. Reality is not a system of logic; reality is governed by physical principles.

It was primarily the introduction of systems analysis, by Bertrand Russell and his associates, into the Soviet Union, through the Laxenburg, Austria-based International Institute of Applied Systems Analysis (IIASA) that caused the Soviet economy to collapse.

Systems analysis has no way of measuring the effect in an economy of a qualitative increase, or decrease in energy flux density, or in the level of infrastructure, or in the increase, or decrease of the cognitive level of the population. This is because those changes change all the variables in ways that are outside of the "system" being analyzed.

It is the use of system analysis, by substituting systems analysis for real science in closed earth-climate computer models, which leads to the absurd, "all the scientists agree..," or "the science is settled…" in matters like climate change, without any regard to the profound macroscopic physical effects coming from the Solar System and the Galaxy. It is the devotees of systems analysis who believe that you can successfully carry out global depopulation to a permanent equilibrium, without acknowledging the physical impossibility of maintaining such an equilibrium in the real physical universe.

It is the use of systems analysis that encourages the devotees of Russell's logic to believe they can account for all the variables sufficiently to launch a first strike and win a nuclear war. This happens to be the basis of the Prompt Global Strike Doctrine, the current U.S. doctrine for nuclear war. If the human race becomes extinct in the near term because of nuclear war, the stupidity of systems analysis may be one of the most important contributing factors.

The practical man is a stupid man. The reason the practical man is a stupid man, is because he has lost the ability to imagine what could be, or what could have been. The practical man can only know what is, or know "how things work." As society collapses the practical man cannot conceive of how it could be otherwise, let alone believe that it could be possible to alter the course of the collapse of things. Worse, the practical man will assault the visionary who tries to create a better future for the practical man. The Twentieth Century is the century of the emergence of the practical man, as made stupid by Bertrand Russell.

How Bertrand Russell Made Us Fearful

The potential for humanity to enter into a nuclear age, far superseding the age of the chemical industrial revolution, began in the early Twentieth Century with the work of individuals such as Madame Curie, Albert Einstein, Max Planck, and others. Over one hundred years later, though the nuclear age is with us in part, the full promise of the nuclear age has not been anywhere near realized. Instead, North America's, Europe's and Japan's populations are dominated by an unscientific hysterical fear of nuclear power and science in general. How did this happen? It happened because of Bertrand Russell.

As World War II was coming to a close, Franklin Delano Roosevelt died. His successor, Harry Truman, followed the advice of the British Empire, advice in which Bertrand Russell had a major influence. That advice was to lead to the dropping of nuclear bombs on

Russell proposed the pre-emptive use of nuclear bombs on the Soviet Union to compel the Soviets to submit to a world government. Here, a nuclear test explosion.

Hiroshima and Nagasaki. This bombing was unnecessary and was done to terrorize the world. Japan was already negotiating a surrender through private channels.

With the dropping of the atomic bombs and the launching of the Cold War, both of which Russell had a major part in, Russell became an advocate of three movements.

• The first was a movement to convince the United States to use their nuclear advantage over the Soviet Union to establish a world government by pre-emptive use of nuclear weapons on the Soviet Union.

• The second was, in the event that the Soviets were able to acquire nuclear weapons before the United States could be convinced, the creation of a movement to convince the Soviet Union to become partners with the United States in a world government.

• The third was to launch a world-wide peace movement to "ban the bomb," using the fear of nuclear war to begin vilifying nuclear power and science in general.

This entire strategy was put forward in a six-page document by Russell which was published Oct. 1, 1946 in the *Bulletin of the Atomic Scientists*, entitled "The Atomic Bomb and the Prevention of War." In that document the entire following 70 years were foretold, including the crisis the world is in now. The following are some of the features of that document:

Since the Soviet Union did develop atomic weapons before the United States was able to have the means to sufficiently, pre-emptively, use nuclear weapons against the Soviet Union, Russell describes the nuclear and technological arms race that would ensue. In Russell's view, one of the main collateral benefits of the nuclear arms race would be the need for secrecy. Such secrecy and extreme security was seen by Russell as a means to compartmentalize and thereby contain, as well as suppress, the dissemination of science to the rest of the world. This is how Russell proposed controlling science and scientists, or in Russell's own words: "It will be necessary to keep their location secret, which will mean virtually a prison camp for those who work in connection with them. It will involve a constant suspicion of treachery … It will involve a complete cessation of freedom for all scientific workers whose activities have any bearing on the war-like utilization of nuclear energy."

Throughout the document, Russell asserts that peace can only come through the installation of a world government. Until that world government comes into place, Russell says, the threat of annihilation through nuclear war will not only always be present, but given human nature, nuclear war would ultimately become inevitable. It is in this document that Russell makes clear that this terror, the terror of nuclear war, is the most efficient means for controlling the world and its politics. It is only for this reason that Bertrand Russell considers the advent of nuclear power to have any good to it. Rather than a belief in progress, as characterized by Franklin Roosevelt's intention, it is the fear of nuclear war which Russell establishes as the controlling feature of the post-World War II period. It is the use and manipulation of this fear that has defined everything that has happened since the death of FDR and the Cold War, to the present current emerging nuclear confrontation between NATO and Russia.

With the establishment of the Pugwash Conference, which began in the mid-1950s, in which Henry Kissinger and many others like him were involved, Bertrand Russell set the stage for establishing the doctrine of Mutually Assured Destruction. This is where the populations of nations are held hostage to nuclear war as a means to keep the peace. It was Bertrand Russell who

Russell addresses the Campaign for Nuclear Disarmament in Trafalgar Square in 1959. He used the fear of nuclear war to vilify nuclear power and science in general.

played a key role in initiating the actions of Nikita Khrushchov which led to the Cuban missile crisis. The Cuban missile crisis was used to terrorize the world, especially for those born after World War II. Those born after World War II, the "baby boomers," were at that time children, or young adolescents, who did not have the emotional maturity to deal with this terror. As a result, an indelible imprint of sheer terror has warped the minds and souls of the generation now entering retirement.

This terror, deep in the psyche of the "boomers," has been extended to everything scientific, especially to nuclear power, whose extensive future use is our future, if we are to have a future. This was a key aspect of what Ronald Reagan's LaRouche-initiated Strategic Defense Initiative was designed to change, by creating with the Soviet Union the joint venture of developing the technologies of defense that would make nuclear missiles obsolete. The combination of the end of the era of nuclear terror, and the benefit of the new technologies created, could have begun an economic and scientific renaissance. This did not happen. Why? It did not happen because the then-incoming Soviet leadership under Yuri Andropov, had been heavily influenced by Bertrand Russell and systems analysis, and because of that, Andropov rejected this incredible opportunity to get out from under the hellish world that Bertrand Russell had created for us.

Most importantly, this terror has created a sense that at any time the future will end. That leaves only the present in which to live. As a result, the "boomers" and the subsequent generations after the "boomers" have ceased to orient themselves to a future that may not exist. In this context, it is the perpetuation of the permanent threat of nuclear annihilation that is the continuing, most significant corrosive psychological factor in destroying the morality of the individual in our society.

This was Bertrand Russell's intention, to keep us in such perpetual fear, that in order to escape that fear, we had to abandon any concern for future generations. But after freeing ourselves from the burden of the future, we have no reason to exist, other than to exist for our momentary experiences. That doesn't give us much to exist for. This has shaped the psyche of our population in North America and Europe to such a degree that there is no way for most people to visualize a future other than the implicit coming doom that we are trying not to think about.

As a result, the West has lost its passion for progress. It has lost its passion for a better future. The brutal assassination of Kennedy and King, wherein a frail glitter of the future still existed, along with the Vietnam War consolidated a malaise which is the core of what afflicts us today. That affliction has a name: Bertrand Russell.

How Bertrand Russell Made Us Evil: Why We Hate the Human Race

It is quite probable that a large minority, if not the majority of North Americans and Europeans, given their decline into degeneracy under the influence of Bertrand Russell, hate humanity and would like to see the human race exterminated. This view is probably more prevalent among the most educated parts of those regions. The only problem that this large minority, or majority, would have with exterminating the human race is purely personal. This view is widely expressed in the culture and in many current practices. It is expressed in everything from the very popular statement, subscribed to almost universally, that "the world is overpopulated, and population needs to be reduced;" to the environmentalist movement's view of humanity as a blight on "mother nature," a blight which "mother nature" will soon eliminate; to the religious fundamentalists who are waiting for the extermination of hated mankind in the end times (except, of course, the chosen); to the explicit death-worship in much of the popular culture; to the plethora of mass shootings; and to the rapidly expanding suicide and drug epidemics. This hatred of humanity was virulently expressed by Bertrand Russell:

• "I hate the world and almost all the people in it. I hate the Labour Congress and the journalists who send men to be slaughtered, and the fathers who feel a smug pride when their sons are killed, and even the pacifists who keep saying human nature is essentially good, in spite of all the daily proofs to the contrary. I hate the planet and the human race—I am ashamed to belong to such a species." *Letter to Colette*, Dec. 28, 1916.

"I hate the world and almost all the people in it. ... I hate the planet and the human race. I am ashamed to belong to such a species," wrote Russell to Colette (Lady Constance Malleson) in 1916, expressing the view he sought to propagate.

• "How much good it would do if one could exterminate the human race." A characteristic saying of Russell, reported in a letter of 8 October 1917 to Lady Ottoline Morrell, by Huxley (p. 395); *Bibliography of Bertrand Russell* (Routledge, 2013).

• "I have been merely oppressed by the weariness and tedium and vanity of things lately: nothing stirs me, nothing seems worth doing or worth having done: the only thing that I strongly feel worth while would be to murder as many people as possible so as to diminish the amount of consciousness in the world..." *Letter to Gilbert Murray*, March 21, 1903.

This hatred of humanity is not shared by the rest of the world outside of North America and Europe. China, Russia, India, the rest of Asia, South America, and Africa do not share this view. Despite the depredations of war, colonialism, and other horrors, the people of these regions want a future, the future that Bertrand Russell wished to prevent.

For that reason, what has emerged there is a new economic system committed to this future, centered on China, Russia, and India, which is now being implemented. This is something that the Bertrand Russell still living in us will not tolerate. This is why, as a last resort, we can be expected, given the Bertrand Russell in us, to support, at least in spirit, the launching of nu-clear war against these nations because they *do* wish to develop and have a future; because they *do* wish to develop nuclear power; because they *do* want to improve the conditions of life for their people; because they *do* believe humanity is essentially good; and most of all because they *do* have the happiness in seeking to bring that future into being that we no longer have.

Why do we hate the human race? We hate the human race because we have allowed Bertrand Russell's hatred of humanity to penetrate the very essence of our being. This is how we were made evil.

Extirpating the Ghost of Bertrand Russell Through the Revival of Classical Culture

For those who are reading this, who have not completely succumbed to spirit of Bertrand Russell, and who, given the circumstances, still miraculously care about the human race, it is time for some serious spiritual house-cleaning. It is also time to become active. It is misery not to become active in this period.

In all of this, the author is recommending the following steps be taken. First, locate in yourself the spirit of the Bertrand Russell movement. Second, extirpate that spirit by becoming involved in classical music and classical culture, and also in the political process which does represent a future. This is what the LaRouche movement is reviving in New York City with what is called the "Manhattan Project." Try to find others who want to do the same. Contact the LaRouche movement at its various locations to see where you can fit into this. Classical music in particular does not involve logic. Classical music is not stupid. Its creators, like Bach and Beethoven, were real scientists. Their creating of classical music involves the kind of methods that are the same as the methods involved in making scientific discoveries. Discovering classical music is in essence discovering your own mind, not the mind of Bertrand Russell.

BOOK REVIEW

Living the Unthinkable

by Jeffrey Steinberg

My Journey at the Nuclear Brink
by William J. Perry
Stanford University Press, 2015
278 pages with illustrations, hardcover,
paperback, and Kindle, from $24.95

Jan 24—Former Secretary of Defense William James Perry (1994-1997) has spent his entire adult life living under the shadow of potential thermonuclear Armageddon. For Perry, it is a deeply personal fact of life, partly as the result of his own choices of career path, partly as the result of being in critical places at critical times.

The net effect is that the former defense industry executive, nuclear weapons analyst, and two-time Defense Department executive has come to believe that the world today is closer to thermonuclear war than at almost any time during the half-century of Cold War between the United States and the Soviet Union. He finds this reality to be alarming beyond description, and he candidly admits that this situation is the consequence of policy decisions by American and NATO leaders that sabotaged the prospects of genuine partnership between the United States and post-Soviet Russia at critical moments during the 1990s and 2000s.

Secretary Perry cannot be described as "soft on Russia." Some of his criticisms of Russian policies are harshly inaccurate, in the same way that he is patently wrong in his characterizations of Ronald Reagan's Strategic Defense Initiative (SDI). In the latter case, I believe he was simply ignorant of the fact that President Reagan, despite his "Evil Empire" rhetoric, was genu-ine in his offer to Moscow of a joint development of a global system of ballistic missile defense that could lead to an era of Mutually Assured Survival.

In fairness to Perry, his misunderstanding of the SDI process was likely colored by his close relationship to Reagan's Secretary of State George Shultz, his Stanford University colleague, who always viewed the Strategic Defense Initiative as a bargaining chip to be traded off in exchange for Soviet ballistic missile and nuclear weapons reductions. Shultz was furious when President Reagan refused to capitulate to his and Mikhail Gorbachov's demands at the 1986 Reykjavik summit, that he abandon SDI and simply agree to nuclear weapon reductions.

Perry was, furthermore, clearly unaware of the role played by Lyndon LaRouche and some of his close colleagues in pursuing back-channel dialogue with Soviet officials throughout 1981-1983 in pursuit of an agreement on collaborative missile defense.

Throughout the book, Perry extolled the virtues of maintaining constant lines of communication with Moscow (and with Beijing), taking full advantage of private Track II channels of dialogue, when government-to-government relations hit an impasse or crisis. Since leaving government, Perry has devoted most of his time to precisely this kind of personal diplomacy, particularly with Russia and North Korea.

These shortcomings are minor, however, when taken in the context of the whole of the message that comes across in his memoir, *My Journey at the Nuclear Brink*. For Perry, preventing the outbreak of a thermonuclear war of extinction is the first and overriding priority. He worries about the danger of an accidental incident triggering an escalation to all-out thermonuclear exchange.

For this reason, he and some of his closest collaborators, like former U.S. Senators Sam Nunn and Richard Lugar, as well as retired Gen. James Cartwright, insist that the United States and Russia should take their nuclear arsenals off of "launch on warning."

Under launch on warning, both sides in the thermonuclear Armageddon process launch all-out retaliatory strikes at the first indication of a first-strike launch by the other. Perry frets that, in the age of cyber warfare, and with U.S.-Russian tensions back in the fore, launch on warning is a virtual guarantee of a thermonuclear exchange at the strategic annihilation level.

Perry's Personal Journey

Perry chose, appropriately, to begin his account in the Fall of 1962, when he received a telephone call at his home from Albert "Bud" Wheelon, then the head of the CIA's Office of Scientific Intelligence and the Chairman of the Guided Missile and Astronautics Intelligence Committee, a high-level top secret inter-governmental commission that oversaw the monitoring of Soviet nuclear weapon and ballistic missile programs. Perry and Wheelon had served on a number of top secret government panels dealing with the Soviet nuclear capabilities.

Wheelon asked Perry to drop all of his work at Stanford University and at the Electronic Defense Labs of Sylvania/GTE to come immediately to Washington. When Perry arrived the next day, he was shown some of the reconnaissance photographs of the Soviet missile installations on Cuba. Perry had been brought in on the American side of the Cuban Missile Crisis.

For the next eight days, Perry, along with Wheelon and a team of nuclear weapons and missile specialists and photography analysts, did hour-by-hour assessments of the Soviet progress on installing deployable nuclear weapons in Cuba.

The close proximity to the Cuban Missile Crisis had a profound impact on Perry, who was 35 years old at the time. He would recount in his memoir that he later found out that, at the height of the crisis, Soviet submarine commanders carrying nuclear weapons had been given authority to launch nuclear weapons without clearance from Moscow, due to communications difficulties. One Soviet submarine commander had to be

National Security Archive

The Cuban Missile Crisis was one of Perry's "up close and personal" encounters with the danger of nuclear war. Here, an Oct. 25, 1962, U.S. surveillance photo showing construction of a Soviet missile site in Cuba.

dissuaded by other officers from launching a nuclear-armed torpedo at a U.S. warship trailing the Soviet ship convoy steaming towards Cuba.

The Cuban Missile Crisis was by no means Perry's first "up close and personal" encounter with the danger of nuclear war. In 1946, at the age of 19, Perry had enlisted in the U.S. Army. He joined the Army Reserve as an officer several years later, and was sent to Japan in 1950, as part of the U.S. Occupation, where he saw, firsthand, the devastation of the American firebombing of Tokyo, and the worse devastation of the Atomic Bomb attack on Hiroshima.

Perry completed his B.S. and M.A. from Stanford University and went on to get his Ph.D. in mathematics from Penn State University (he was born and raised in Pennsylvania).

It was the height of the Cold War and the tail end of the McCarthy Red Scare, when a vast majority of Americans were terrified about their job security and the specter of the Red purges. With his advanced degrees in mathematics, Perry was one of those Americans who was drawn into the Cold War drama as part of the privileged segment that were given security clearances to work in the growing American military-industrial complex.

From 1954-1964, Perry worked for the Electronic Defense Labs of Sylvania/GTE in northern California.

He worked on detailed analysis of Soviet missile systems, assessing their accuracy, distance, and potential throw-weight on a number of programs administered by the Pentagon.

In 1964, Perry left Sylvania/GTE to go off on his own, with a number of co-workers. They founded Electromagnetic Systems Lab (ESL), a firm that similarly did highly classified technical work for the Pentagon, both in evaluating Soviet systems and developing counter-systems. Perry was President of ESL, frequently commuting back to Washington for secret consultations at the Pentagon.

In 1977, Perry was summoned to Washington by Harold Brown, one of his close associates on some of the top secret Pentagon panels. Brown had been named Secretary of Defense by the newly elected President Jimmy Carter, and Brown asked Perry to take the job of Under Secretary of Defense for Research and Engineering, a post that would put him in the very center of American work on bolstering deterrents against possible Soviet nuclear attack. Perry reluctantly took the job, serving out the full Carter term in office.

Perry's number one priority as Assistant Secretary of Defense was the Soviet nuclear weapons threat, which he worked on tirelessly. Perry was credited at this time with developing a strategy to offset Soviet advantages through asymmetric U.S. capabilities. Perry found, as soon as he arrived in Washington, that, as the Soviets achieved parity with the United States on strategic nuclear weapons and ICBMs, the United States was increasing its reliance on tactical nuclear weapons, to deter a Soviet ground invasion of Western Europe. He thought that this idea of tactical nuclear weapons in Europe was madness. Along with Harold Brown, Perry put the top Pentagon scientists to work on the original development of stealth technology, reasoning that if the United States had the ability to penetrate Soviet air defenses, it would offset the Soviet conventional advantage over NATO in Europe, without posing the immediate risk of nuclear war triggered by U.S. use of tactical nuclear weapons to block a Soviet conventional move. The result was the F-117 stealth bomber.

During that tenure in the Carter Administration, Perry also promoted the development of "smart" conventional weapons, as another means of abandoning the reliance on tactical nuclear weapons in Europe.

The third prong of his "offset" strategy was the investment in the Global Positioning Satellite (GPS) system, a program that had fierce resistance from within the Office of Management and Budget (OMB) and on Capitol Hill. Perry won that battle with a few small compromises, and GPS went ahead.

After Carter's re-election defeat, Perry returned to Stanford University, but continued to serve on Pentagon study boards, including the Packard Commission on defense acquisition reforms.

When Bill Clinton was elected President in the 1992 elections, Perry was summoned back to Washington, this time as Deputy Secretary of Defense under Les Aspin. By now the Soviet Union and the Warsaw Pact had dissolved, and one of the great concerns in those harrowing transitional days was the danger of loose nuclear weapons or fuel getting in the wrong hands.

In 1992, Congress had passed and President George H.W. Bush had signed the Cooperative Threat Reduction Act of 1972, otherwise known as the Nunn-Lugar Act, named after the two Senators who had co-sponsored the bill. Under Nunn-Lugar, the United States pledged to fund programs in the former Soviet states to dismantle and secure the vast arsenal of nuclear warheads, enriched uranium, and ICBMs. Many of those systems were stored in post-Soviet independent states, including Ukraine and Kazakhstan, with few resources to secure or dismantle those systems.

On Dec. 15, 1993, Perry was in Moscow, participating in a meeting of the Gore-Chernomyrdin Commission. Deputy Secretary of State Strobe Talbot pulled Perry aside to tell him that the President had asked for Aspin's resignation, over the "Black Hawk Down" incident in Somalia. The President nominated Adm. Bobby Ray Inman, former director of the National Security Agency (NSA) and Deputy Director of the CIA as Aspin's replacement.

But after a torrent of neoconservative media attacks on the retired four star Admiral, Inman announced he was withdrawing his name from the nomination. President Clinton, at Inman's urging, named Perry as the new Secretary of Defense. Perry and Inman had been close collaborators during the Carter years when Perry was at Defense and Inman was at the NSA. Inman told President Clinton that Perry was the only person capable of achieving the urgently needed procurement reforms and other crucial changes in the U.S. military posture, during the period of "peace dividends" after the fall of the Warsaw Pact.

Perry did succeed in pushing ahead with the Nunn-Lugar dismantling of all of the former Soviet nuclear weapons located outside Russia, and was able to do it in

Secretary of Defense Perry worked closely with military officials of Russia and the newly independent states to dismantle nuclear arsenals outside Russia in the 1990s. Here, Perry (right) clasps hands with Ukraine Defense Minister Valeriy Shmarov (center) and Russian Defense Minister Gen. Pavel Grachev (left), as they plant sunflowers where a missile silo had been.

close partnership with the Russian Ministry of Defense and armed forces.

Perry focused on outreach to Russia and the former Warsaw Pact countries, promoting the Partnership for Peace, while opposing NATO expansion, until the United States and Russia had achieved a durable and lasting partnership. In his memoir and in other recent writings and speeches, he has continued to hold the United States and NATO responsible for the collapse of collaboration with Russia. Some of the most poignant segments of his book deal with his close working with Russian military officials in the dismantling of the Soviet nuclear arsenals spread across the former Warsaw Pact and Soviet Union states that were now independent, and going through hard economic times.

Perry saved special harsh words for President George W. Bush and Vice President Dick Cheney, for their cancellation of all negotiations with North Korea, from the moment they came into office in Jan. 2001.

Although Perry had left the Clinton Administration after the first term to return to Stanford University, he remained active in Washington diplomacy and particularly on the North Korea front. In Clinton's second term, he served on a commission that visited Pyongyang several times, to revive the 1994 nuclear disarmament agreement. By Perry's eyewitness account, in 2000, as the result of persistent diplomacy, the United States and North Korea were about to sign a landmark

agreement, formally ending the Korean War and assuring that North Korea's plutonium program, a potential nuclear weapons program, would be dismantled with tight international supervision.

At that time, North Korea had no nuclear bombs, and was prepared to forego future nuclear weapons, in return for normalization of relations with the United States and U.S. regional allies. It was a "win-win" situation which was shut down the day that Bush and Cheney took over the White House. Today, North Korea is believed to have a small arsenal of nuclear weapons, and delivery systems that can reach targets in the region.

It is these kinds of failures of sane diplomacy that have convinced Perry that he must take a stand, beyond his low-profile, throughout his career in government.

In the past months, Perry has been more vocal and public about his concerns that Obama Administration policies are driving a dangerous wedge between the United States and the Russians, and the ultimate consequences of these policy disasters could be nuclear Armageddon. Perry has appeared on television, at public events, and at book events all over the country, and his message is always the same: The United States and Russia must find a path for de-escalating the conflict and reviving the spirit of true collaboration around common objectives.

It is clear that his decision to write his memoirs, and to write them with the points of emphasis that he chose, is the most significant contribution he is making to the prevention of a thermonuclear war. As a member of the World War II generation, who served in the armed forces and then went into the world of security clearances, top secret intelligence, and nuclear war planning, he has approached his war-prevention intervention with a degree of humility and under-statement, which makes his dire warnings today about the imminent danger of thermonuclear war all the more powerful.

William Perry is the kind of person to be taken in dead seriousness, when he says that thermonuclear Armageddon is closer now than at any time in his 89 years on Earth.

Every Day Counts In Today's Showdown To Save Civilization

That's why you need EIR's **Daily Alert Service**, a strategic overview compiled with the input of Lyndon LaRouche, and delivered to your email 5 days a week.

For example: On Jan. 7, EIR's Daily Alert featured the British hand behind the pattern of global provocations toward war. Of special note is British Intelligence's role in instigating the Saudi Kingdom's attempt to set off a Sunni-Shia war. This religious war has been the intent of British strategy since the Blair-Bush attack on Iraq in 2003.

We also uniquely update you regularly on the progress toward the release of the suppressed 28 pages of the Congressional Inquiry on 9/11, which would expose the Saudi role.

Every edition highlights the reality of the impending financial crash/bail-in policies that would realize the British goal of mass depopulation.

This is intelligence you need to act on, if we are going to survive as a nation and a species. Can you really afford to be without it?

THURSDAY, JANUARY 7, 2016

Volume 2, Number 97

EIR Daily Alert Service

P.O. Box 17390, Washington, DC 20041-0390

- British Crown Pushing War and Genocide in 2016
- Financial Mudslide Goes On; Monetarist Tyranny Gloats over Bail-Ins
- Moody's Downgrades Portugal's Novo Banco
- Puerto Rico's Default: It's Every Vulture for Himself
- Wide Glass-Steagall Debate Set Off Again by Sanders Speech
- MI6 Mouthpiece Evans-Pritchard Touts Persian Gulf Chaos
- North Korea Tests a Miniaturized Hydrogen Bomb
- Uighur Terrorists Found in Indonesia
- Foreign Investors Are Flocking In to China

EDITORIAL

British Crown Pushing War and Genocide in 2016

Xi Extends Belt and Road To War-Torn Mideast

by William Jones

Jan. 24—On a ground-breaking visit to three major countries in the Middle East—Saudi Arabia, Egypt, and Iran—from January 19 to 23, President Xi Jinping brought to this war-torn region a message of hope and optimism, through his commitment to revitalize the Middle East by linking China's plan for a New Silk Road with these, the countries of the ancient Silk Road. This move now promises to overturn the rules that have hitherto prevailed in the region, long a playground of British financial interests, one which they have used to keep the world destabilized and on the brink of war.

While China has long had interests here, receiving much of its oil and gas from the Middle East, it has kept a low political profile in an area long dominated by Britain and the United States. During the Bush-Obama regimes, the entire region has been subject to a major destabilization that has created chaos and devastation in its wake, with the potential for leading to a new world war. Following on Russian President Putin's historic intervention against terrorism begun last Sept. 30, the high-level Chinese intervention has the potential to turn the situation completely around.

In an article published in the UAE newspaper *Al-Ittihad*, author Mohammed Aref expresses the sense of optimism engendered by the visit. "China is redrawing the map of the

world, turning the seven continents into six by making Asia and Europe one continent," he wrote. In the article, Aref also notes the key role of the "Silk Road Lady," Helga Zepp-LaRouche, in spearheading what is now the main thrust of China's foreign policy, to which she has given the name, the New Silk Road.

But this New Silk Road, or what the Chinese call the Silk Road Economic Belt and the Twenty-first Century Maritime Silk Road, is not simply a project for economic cooperation, but rather is a new paradigm for relations between sovereign nations. The strategic significance of the Silk Road narrative is not lost on the

Xinhua/Ju Peng

Xi Jinping wears the Abdulaziz Medal he has just been awarded by Saudi King Salman bin Abdulaziz Al Saud.

countries visited by the Chinese President. The old Silk Road, dating back 2,000 years, was in many respects a Golden Age for the countries of the Middle East and Central Asia. While Europe was immersed in the Dark Ages, there was a flourishing of culture, art, and science in the great capitals of Central Asia and the Middle East. In fact, it was through Latin translations of Arabic works, often by Jewish scholars in places like Andalusian Spain, that the first glimmerings of the literary and scientific work of the ancient Greeks were made known to the West. In that era, China and the countries of Iran, Egypt, and the Arabian Peninsula were involved in a great union of trade and cultural exchanges. The message of the Chinese President is that that era can be revived with Twenty-first Century methods.

Arabic Daily Hails Zepp-LaRouche's Role In New Silk Road

Jan. 21 (EIRNS)—The Arabic-language newspaper *Al-Ittihad* in the United Arab Emirates published a column by Mohammed Aref, a science and technology consultant, on Chinese President Xi Jinping's visit to Saudi Arabia, Egypt, and Iran, congratulating the New Silk Road Lady—Helga Zepp-LaRouche—and the Schiller Institute for this new visionary policy.

Mohammed Aref

The column, titled "China's 51st Century" (according to China's record of its history), gives a poetic and exciting image of the tour by President Xi to the region and of China's emphasis on the New Silk Road and economic development in its policy declaration.

In 1997, Aref was the first Arab journalist to write a full-page review of *EIR*'s first Eurasian Land-Brige Report, in the London-based Arabic daily *Al-Hayat*, of which he was the Scientific Editor.

After debunking the argument that China's economy is in decline, Aref states: "China is redrawing the map of the world, turning the seven continents into six by making Asia and Europe one continent. 'Let the world be, for no one can succeed in conquering the world and changing it,' as the Chinese saying goes, and as expressed by the Chinese Foreign Ministry Arab Policy Paper which was issued last week, in which is revived the Silk Road, which used to link Chinese with the Arab world for more than 2,000 years. The road of Chinese wisdom is like the a 'Silk Road' which connects the greatest continental Asian-European landmass, and extends to the shores of the Pacific, Indian, and Atlantic oceans through infrastructure for agriculture, industry, trade, technology, science and culture."

In his concluding paragraph, Aref reports Zepp-LaRouche's historic role:

"'The Arab-Asian Land-Bridge: The Pulsating Heart of the New Silk Road' was the title of my report in a London newspaper in November 1997, and I never imagined then that this project, which was designed by the Schiller Institute, would be adopted by China and that the Chinese President would bring it with him to the Arab region this week. Last September, Beijing celebrated the release of the Chinese translation of the new report, 'The Silk Road Becomes the World Land-Bridge.' In the next month the Arabic translation of the report will be published, and is prepared by Hussein Askary, the Iraqi member of the Schiller Institute, which was established by the German Academician Helga LaRouche, who is called by the Chinese 'The Silk Road Lady,' because she paved the way for the New Silk Road through hundreds of conferences and scientific and political seminars, and she 'established the concept of the Eurasian Land-Bridge as a war prevention tool,' according to the Chinese Scholar Deng Yifan. Helga LaRouche and China are like the woman, about whom the Chinese proverb states: 'The female always surpasses the male by her calmness, and she becomes fruitful even in her silence.' And the other proverb: The Great Country is like the lower part of the river, where the earth of the world meets the female of the world [*Daodejing*, Chapter 61—ed.]."

Aref's column is here.

Xinhua/Wang Ye

Iranian President Hassan Rouhani presents Xi Jinping at the welcoming ceremony in Tehran.

China Issues Arab Policy Paper

Prior to Xi's departure for the Middle East, the Chinese Foreign Ministry issued an "Arab Policy Paper," the first of its kind, which outlined an agenda for cooperation with the region. The occasion of the publication was the 60th anniversary this year of the establishment of diplomatic relations with an Arab country, Egypt. But the paper would also provide the groundwork for Xi's visit.

"Over the past 60 years," the paper says, "China-Arab friendly cooperation has made historic leaps in breadth and depth. It has become a model of South-South cooperation and gained the following successful experience: Both sides have always respected and treated each other as equals and remain brothers, friends, and partners no matter what happens on the world arena; both sides have insisted on the principle of mutual benefit, win-win, and common development, and have pursued common interest and sustainable development no matter what changes or developments take place on either side; and both sides have promoted dialogue, exchanges, and mutual learning among civilizations, and have always respected each other's social system and development path no matter what differences exist in ideology."

It is precisely such a relationship, based on mutual

respect, that China has been attempting to build with its neighbors in the "One Belt, One Road" strategy. The interventionism and unilateralism practiced by the Bush and Obama administrations, dictated by their British game-masters, has caused havoc in the region. Establishing peace requires a new paradigm in international relations, and this is what China is trying to establish.

In Saudi Arabia, the first stop on his trip, Xi witnessed the signing of fourteen agreements, including agreements on oil production and nuclear energy, and an agreement to work toward a free-trade agreement with the countries of the Gulf Cooperation Council (GCC) by the end of 2016. In Saudi Arabia, President Xi met with Saudi King Salman bin Abdulaziz al Saud, Saudi Crown Prince Mohamed bin Salman, the speaker of the Majlis (Consultative Council), and the head of the GCC.

Suez Canal—A Silk Road Hub

The second stop on Xi's trip was Egypt. China has increased its cooperation with the country since President Abdel Fatah al-Sisi took power and re-established some order in a situation that was quickly spinning out of control under the Muslim Brotherhood president, Mohamed Morsi. China views Egypt as a major hub on the Belt and Road, with the newly improved and expanded Suez Canal now able to service a much larger amount of expected shipping from the Asia-Pacific region.

In an article published in *Al-Ahram*, the major Egyptian daily, prior to his visit, President Xi outlined a development perspective: "The aspiration of the Arab people for a better life not only provides the momentum for reform, it also lays the foundation for regional stability." "By jointly developing the Belt and Road Initiative," Xi wrote, "the two sides can link up our respective development strategies, [and] deepen and expand cooperation in energy, trade and investment, infrastructure and high technology. China welcomes Egypt and other Arab countries to get on board the fast train of its development and hopes that our respective development and growth could be well-aligned and mutually reinforcing." The two sides signed 21 trade agreements, including a broad five-year cooperation agreement. These included agreements on cooperation in civil aviation, electricity, higher education and science, media, banking, and trade. China will invest $15 billion in Egypt in infrastructure projects, including a China-Egypt Suez Economic and Trade Cooperation Zone, which is slated to provide employment to 10,000 Egyptian workers. China will also invest in the construction of a new Egyptian capital city just east of present-day Cairo.

Xinhua/Pan Chaoyue

Chinese President Xi brought to the war-torn Middle East a message of hope, the New Silk Road. Here, a refugee takes a walk in downtown Homs, Syria.

In Cairo, President Xi also gave an important speech to the Arab League in which he underlined the thrust of his policy for the region as a whole. "The key to overcoming difficulties is to accelerate development," Xi told the members of the League. "Turmoil in the Middle East stems from the lack of development, and the ultimate solution will depend on development, which bears on everyone's well-being and dignity. It is a race against time and a struggle between hope and disillusion. Only when young people are able to live a fulfilled life with dignity through development can hope prevail in their heart. Only then will they voluntarily reject violence, extremist ideologies, and terrorism." Xi also reiterated China's support for an Israel-Palestine two-state solution and the creation of a viable Palestinian state with its 1967 borders.

President al-Sisi also hosted the Chinese President on a tour of the Luxor Temple, more than 3,400 years old, stressing the relationship of these two ancient cultures. Both presidents viewed performances under the stars at Luxor by both Chinese and Egyptian performers.

Long-Term Agreement With Iran

Finally, President Xi visited Iran, the first head of state to do so in the aftermath of the signing of the P-5 nuclear agreement with Iran, in which China was a key participant. Iran, especially, has its own history as a key country along the ancient Silk Road. Many of the surviving documents and contracts from the old Silk Road period were written in languages stemming from old Persian and much of the culture of the ancient Silk Road was also Persian.

In an article by the Chinese President published in the Iranian newspapers a day before he arrived, Xi wrote: "Over 2,000 years ago during the Western Han Dynasty in China, the Chinese envoy Zhang Qian's deputy came to Iran and received a warm welcome. Seven centuries later, during the Tang and Song dynasties, many Iranians came to China's Xi'an and Guangzhou to study, practice medicine, and do business. In the Thirteenth Century, the famous Iranian poet Saadi wrote about his unforgettable travel to Kashgar, Xinjiang. In the Fifteenth Century, a renowned Chinese navigator, Zheng He, from the Ming Dynasty, led seven maritime expeditions, which took him to Hormuz in southern Iran three times."

More recently, China has had a long-standing economic relationship with Iran since 1971, which was not curtailed during the days in which economic sanctions kept other countries away. While 140 countries have now sent delegations to Tehran, eager to cut deals with the Islamic Republic of Iran, the Chinese still maintain something of a special status with Iran. This was particularly stressed by Supreme Leader Ayatollah Ali Khamenei who, in his meeting with the Chinese President, said that Iran still mistrusted the West, but that China was seen as an old friend. The two countries signed an unprecedented 25-year Comprehensive Cooperation Agreement coordinating the two nations' respective development agendas. They also signed a Memorandum of Understanding on Jointly Promoting the Silk Road Economic Belt and the Twenty-first Century Maritime Silk Road.

Iran and China signed seventeen documents for cooperation in economic, industrial, cultural, and judicial fields, including an agreement between Iranian and Chinese nuclear chiefs for peaceful energy cooperation. Others agreements involved environmental cooperation, financing of a bullet train railway, and banking cooperation. President Rouhani called this a "new chapter" in the two countries' relationship.

The visit of the Chinese President to the Middle East has indeed signaled a "new chapter" in the history of the Middle East. The historic decision by Russian President Vladimir Putin to help Syria fight terrorism, successfully judoed attempts by Obama and the British to launch war in Europe and begin a new round of "color revolutions" in the Mideast. Now, the visit of the Chinese President has provided the basis for a new paradigm in relations among nations, based on the mutual interests of them all, and a revival of those elements of their cultures which represented a high point for humanity. As the New Silk Road will be traveled more rapidly by high-speed rail than was the ancient road by camel, the great values of cooperation and mutual benefit characteristic of the old Silk Road can be transmitted more rapidly on the new one. If the project is brought to fruition, these nations—which provided such an important role in the advance of human civilization 2,000 years ago—can again make a valuable contribution to the development of mankind on our planet, launching a new Renaissance for humanity.

China's New Silk Road Policy Is the Solution to the Refugee Crisis!

by Helga Zepp-LaRouche

The author is chairwoman of the German political party Civil Rights Solidarity Movement. Her article is translated from German.

Jan. 23—Whereas on the public side of this year's World Economic Forum in Davos, the well-heeled Establishment held forth as usual on an eclectic array of topics, and private conversations behind-the-scenes were dominated chiefly by panic over the escalating financial crash of the trans/Atlantic sector, Chinese President Xi Jinping did something much more important: With a spectacular trip to Saudi Arabia, Egypt, and Iran, he laid the basis for the integration of Southwest Asia into the New Silk Road, and thereby created the prerequisite for ending the conflict between Shi'a and Sunni in the region. With the perspective for reconstruction and development offered by China, the concrete opportunity suddenly arises to overcome the refugee crisis by rebuilding the migrants' devastated home countries.

But there was also a surprise at Davos: In the panel titled "The Future of Europe," German Finance Minister Wolfgang Schäuble suddenly advocated a Marshall Plan for the Middle East and Africa. In an inversion of George W. Bush's phrase, he called for "a coalition of the willing," that is, of countries that are willing to invest billions in those regions from which the refugees come. And in a further reversal, Schäuble agreed with Greek Prime Minister Alexis Tsipras, who was sitting at the same dais, that it would be disgraceful to attempt to turn Europe into a fortress, and that pressure on the external borders of the European Union should rather be reduced by such a development perspective.

What are we to make of this? Has Schäuble, of all people—the super-EU European and the bankers' man, the one who demands discipline from Greece, the Troika's spokesman for austerity—suddenly discovered that he has a soft spot for the development of these countries? In any case, France's King Henry IV believed long ago that, for the sake of a good cause, everyone need not be motivated by the highest ideal; some people won't achieve a goal until they feel their own shirts burning. Because Schäuble knows: Without Schengen—the agreement to abolish border controls within the EU—there is no euro, and without the euro there is no EU. Since there is no solidarity in the EU, then it's better not to exert pressure, which only makes the failure of the EU's Lisbon Treaty more obvious, but just count on "the willing."

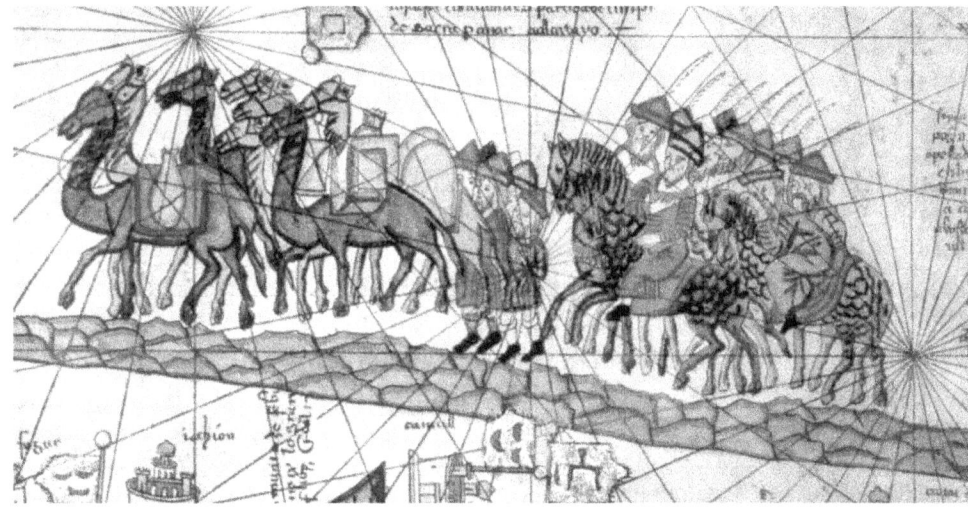

A medieval European rendition of travel on the ancient Silk Road.

Xi Jinping Brings 'Win-Win' Policy to Arab Capitals

But it was Xi Jinping, with his groundbreaking trip to the most populous countries of the Shi'a and Sunni denominations, who created the opening for such a shift. Before his trip, a Chinese Foreign Ministry position paper on China's policy towards the Arab world explicitly referred to the 2,000-year friendship between China and the Arab states from the time of the ancient Silk Road, as the basis for a new model of cooperation for mutual progress. Xi stressed the same principles in his speech to the Arab League in Cairo, in which he emphasized dialogue as the means to settle conflicts and called for respect for the decisions of the peoples of this region, instead of attempting to impose solutions from the outside. All problems, he said, can be overcome only if the happiness of the local people is promoted.

In addition to dozens of agreements with the three countries he visited, worth a total of around $55 billion (!) in the areas of infrastructure, transport, energy, and high technology, as subcomponents of the expansion of the New Silk Road ("One Belt, One Road"), the Chinese President also advanced the entirely new concept of international relations that his China defends. His arrival was preceded by the publication of an article signed by him in the daily newspapers of the respective countries, in which he referred to the best traditions in the culture of that country, such as the interchanges between the Han dynasty and Alexandria in Egypt 2,000 years ago, and the cooperation of Prime Minister Zhou Enlai and President Gamal Abdel Nasser at the Bandung Conference in the struggle against colonialism and hegemony. In his article in an Iranian newspaper, he emphasized the friendly welcome of Chinese emissaries during the Han, Song, and Tang dynasties, as well as the unforgettable journey of the Persian poet Saadi to Kashgar.

A comment in the Egyptian newspaper *Al-Ahram* by Mohamed Fayez Farahat makes it clear that people in these countries understand the totally new quality of the New Silk Road policy. It is one of the largest and most important projects that has ever been proposed in human history, he wrote. In contrast to projects proposed by the West, "which either ended in nothing or projects that unevenly distribute revenues from global

World Economic Forum/swiss-image.ch/Valeriano Di Domenico

German Finance Minister Wolfgang Schäuble at the "Future of Europe" session of the World Economic Forum in Davos, Switzerland.

economic and financial transactions in favor of economically developed countries," and in contrast to all of the Western attempts at exporting democracy, which have completely failed, the Chinese policy is focused on the broadest inclusion of all regions. Thus it is not oriented toward geopolitics, but toward the economic development of the cooperating states, while also making the financing available. Therefore, the New Silk Road very quickly found willingness to cooperate on the part of 60 nations, the Egyptian journalist wrote.

China's proposal for inclusive "win-win" cooperation of all nations on this Earth—on the basis of absolute respect for the sovereignty of all countries and for their chosen political, social, and economic models—with the aim of overcoming the poverty of all, of cooperation in high-technology areas and of cultural exchanges, emphasizing the high points of one another's culture, provides a revolutionary model for the cooperation of mankind, which excludes war as a means of conflict resolution.

This new concept of relations among nations embodies the same higher level of *coincidentia oppositorum*, the coincidence of opposites, expressed in Nicholas of Cusa's work *De Pace Fidei (On the Peace of Faith)*, which he wrote in response to the fall of Constantinople in 1453. The idea is that there is a higher plane and a higher truth in the order of Creation, through which differences can be overcome. This thinking is reflected in China in the idea of the "mandate of heaven" and Confucian philosophy, while in European humanist philosophy, it is expressed in the idea of natural law: that there are natural laws which ultimately are also efficient in the affairs of mankind, and which people must abide by to ensure their continued existence in the long term.

Time Is Running Out

The Chinese model embodies the overcoming of geopolitics, the main cause of two world wars in the Twentieth Century, and the acute danger of a third one—this time the last, because today it would be a thermonuclear world war. Schäuble is right when he says that time is running out—but not only with regard to the refugee crisis, the cohesion of the EU, and the continued existence of the Merkel government. William White, the chairman of the Review Committee of the OECD and former chief economist of the Bank of International Settlements (BIS), also warned dramatically on the eve of the Davos conference, in an interview with the *Daily Telegraph*, that the debt accumulated worldwide over the last eight years is so great that it can no longer be serviced or repaid, "and this will be uncomfortable for a lot of people who think they own assets that are worth something." The only question is whether these debts will be written off in an orderly fashion or go under in chaos, he said.

Of course Schäuble knows that, as Finance Minister. If he is really serious about the Marshall Plan for Southwest Asia and Africa, then he must immediately initiate the Glass-Steagall two-tier banking system throughout Europe, as the only way to write down the banks' toxic paper in an orderly way, and in place of the casino economy, put in place a credit system for development of the real economy, in Southwest Asia and Africa as well as in Germany and the rest of Europe. This is the test of whether his Damascus Road conversion is real.

Chinese Prime Minister Li Keqiang has just spoke with Chancellor Merkel by telephone, and according to the Chinese press agency Xinhua, the two reaffirmed their intention to cooperate in the attempt to overcome the Syrian humanitarian crisis. China is holding out its hand, and we must grasp it now, in order to give the Germans confidence once again and give those in in Southwest Asia and Africa an existence and a future.

There Is Life After the Euro!

Program for an Economic Miracle in Southern Europe, the Mediterranean Region, and Africa

AN **EIR** SPECIAL REPORT

CONTENTS
Introduction by Helga Zepp-LaRouche
Greece, and a Marshall Plan for the Mediterranean Basin
Spain: Bridge to African Development
The Rebirth of Italy's Mezzogiorno
Africa Pass
The Transaqua Project
North Africa: The Blue Revolution
What Europe Can Learn from Argentina
A German Economic Miracle for Europe

http://www.larouchepub.com/special_report/2012/spec_rpt_program_medit.pdf

INTERVIEW

Italian Evangelists of Classical Music in Manhattan

Jan. 7—Two remarkable opera singers who bring Classical music to the younger generation in Italy, Alessio Magnaguagno (bass) and Fausta Ciceroni (soprano), participated in the LaRouches' Manhattan Project in New York in November and December. They discuss that experience and their work in Italy in this interview with Liliana Gorini, chairwoman of Movisol, LaRouche's movement in Italy.

Gorini: On Nov. 7th you sang Verdi arias during a Manhattan Project *Musikabend* to celebrate Friedrich Schiller's 257th birthday in New York. How did you come to be in touch with the Schiller Institute?

The Singers: The opportunity came completely by chance. We were in touch with an Italian association in New York, which was invited to the *Musikabend*, and it gave us the invitation. Since we are both opera singers, we volunteered to sing Verdi arias at the event. Our offer was accepted. We and other artists sang, accompanied on the piano by the wonderful maestro Robert Wilson. It was an emotional experience for us twice over, first of all because of the prestigious audience and excellent pianist, but also because it was the first time we experienced singing at A = 432 hz. It was incredible to feel how natural this tuning is. If we were supporters of the Verdi tuning before, now we are all the more so.

Gorini: You also attended both Manhattan Project performances of Handel's *Messiah* in New York. What is your judgment of the Manhattan Project, and what are your thoughts about the "community chorus" which sang in those concerts? How did the audience respond?

The Singers: We had the opportunity to hear both performances of the *Messiah*, in Brooklyn and Manhattan. The concerts were great; particularly the chorus was sensational. The audience filled the churches and was attentive and respectful, and at the end, applauded warmly. Even if the social and logistical contexts were different for the two concerts, what united both performances was the total concentration of the audience on the music program, and we as part of the audience enjoyed the Verdi tuning. It was very good to see whole families participate in the concert, demonstrating that music can be a bridge between generations, and an occasion to join in sharing the emotions of great art. Many were young people who participated in the event on

Sabrina Ciferri

Bass Alessio Magnaguagno and soprano Fausta Ciceroni in duet.

their own. At the beginning they felt a little awkward, as if they should justify that they were investing two hours of their time in Classical culture. But their applause at the end and the expressions on their faces proved that great works of art have no temporal, generational, or geographic bounds.

Gorini: You seem to have your own Manhattan Project in Rome, thanks to which you have managed, without any help from the Italian government, to stage 35 operas in schools, and you are involving pupils in the performance, after teaching them singing from scratch. Yours is a praiseworthy project, which should be replicated elsewhere, since it brings our opera patrimony to the youngest. How did you get the idea?

The Singers: That is a delicate and interesting question. We come from very different families and backgrounds, but both of our families always believed in the value of learning and knowledge as the only source of true freedom and independence. That is why we had the idea of involving anyone in our passion for opera who was willing to share the same passion, and had the will to improve and learn. We also taught singing to people who had never had the opportunity, and now could be on an opera stage for the first time. Our work in schools was mainly to teach students to listen, because a concert is not only performed by those who are on stage, but also by the audience. One cannot be without the other. And that is what we tried to realize with our project called "Boys and Girls Go to the Opera." Opera goes to the schools and schools go to the opera!

We arrange for the main characters of the planned opera to go to the participating schools to meet the students in their own environment. We explain to them what they will see and hear, and the intent of the composer and librettist. We play some of the composer's compositions, not the opera—something else—so that the students could recognize the compositional method, but without spoiling the surprise of the performance. These "concert lessons" provided an incredible opportunity to explain to them the idea of the opera, enable them to understand the dimension of listening, answer their questions, and bring them to a higher level of par-

Sabrina Ciferri

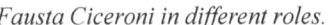

Fausta Ciceroni in different roles.

ticipation. To have 500 young students in a theatre, listening to an opera for three hours and applauding thunderously at the end, is a great reward.

Gorini: Can you give us some example of the operas you have staged in Rome?

The Singers: We went step by step, starting with single act operas such as Pergolesi's *La Serva Padrona (The Servant Turned Mistress)*, Mozart's *Bastian and Bastienne*, Donizetti's *Rita, or The Beaten Husband*, and his *Betly, or The Swiss Chalet*. The success of these operas induced us to move to a more important repertoire, from Mozart's *Cosi Fan Tutte (Women Are Like That)*, to Verdi, Rossini, Donizetti, Bizet, and Puccini. A pleasant memory for sure is Bizet's *Carmen*. The score calls for a chorus of street urchins with white voices [no vibrato, no brilliance—ed.], and we decided to teach it to students at one of the schools. For three months we were at the school twice a week to teach the boys,—first, how to behave in an opera theatre, and then the basics of solfège and singing, until the performance was perfect in intonation and rhythm. And then there was the enthusiasm of these little men who, well aware of their role and their responsibilities, were able to come on stage and perform entirely on their own!

The performances of Magnaguagno and Ciceroni at the Nov. 7 Musikabend in New York may be seen here.

Noble Art, I Thank You!

by Philip Ulanowsky

Du holde Kunst, in wie viel grauen Stunden,
Wo mich des Lebens wilder Kreis umstrickt,
Hast du mein Herz zu warmer Lieb' entzunden,
Hast mich in eine bessre Welt entrückt ...

You, gracious art, in how many grey hours,
When life's wild circle ensnares me,
Have you kindled my heart to ardent love,
Have you borne me into a better world ...[1]

Jan. 15—Among the most difficult challenges for today's wiser parent and teacher, is explaining to our children and youth that what has come to be called normal in society, is in no way normal. They have known nothing else. But, even for those with some memory of a time when not every newscast featured a story about murder, terrorism, the danger to the United States from some small foreign country, or cataclysmic crises in the environment, what are the leading escape routes? To what do even well meaning people turn when they cannot face the economic and social nightmare surrounding them? Are not the predominant entertainments also mainly filled with violence, depravity, corruption, and an inability of even the "good guys" in the popular dramas to do anything except react to each new ghastly event? Isn't this just an escape from the proverbial frying pan into the fire? Have we nothing better?

As soon as we reject the proposal that, really, we are only animals, each of us faces the question, "If not, then, what *am* I, really?"—and it's a good thing to ask. Classical art holds the answer, but not as you may think. Really it's a doorway to your mind.

Popular music (generically speaking) reflects today's culture in general, the one that burns. How does it affect you? Perhaps it's smooth and quiet, and you relax; maybe it's toe-tapping dance music; or, it could be violent and rageful, with or without words—some say it soothes. However you feel, the answer to your true identity will remain obscure until you discover the genius of someone who knows your real mind, the mind you may not realize—or even dare to hope—that you have.

Classical music is our gift from a succession of true geniuses, each opening new potentials from having struggled to master the work of his or her predecessors—Johann Sebastian Bach (1685-1750), for example, mastering and then revolutionizing the art of composition of his day; Wolfgang Mozart (1756-1791) discovering J.S. Bach and developing thoroughly new potentials; Beethoven (1770-1827) working through Bach and Mozart on the way to creating his own revolutions. All this was a kind of science, each discoverer superseding the crucial discoveries of the past. Its purpose? To find a more enveloping, more powerfully unified expression of the universal creativity of the human mind; to honor that which is most noble in humanity, and by so doing, to enlighten more of humanity to its own, great potential.

How can music achieve this? Imagine, instead of musical entertainment, a music that seeks to solve a problem it poses to itself. It poses an irony in the language of tonality—that is, of musical tonal relationships—which, like the physical reality of the living universe whose laws we reflect, is bounded but infinitely developable.

Just as beautiful nature around us in countless ways expresses the action of living harmonies and proportionality in its development, so the musical domain that we call, after J.S. Bach, well-tempered, reflects the higher ordering process of which it was born. It is not a closed system, not a logic. Rather, as great composers invite us to hear, new development possibilities infuse every part of it. As in spoken language, in which dictionary definitions of words do not limit the ideas which they may be chosen to convey, so, in Classical music the potential for new ideas supersedes the limitations of tones.

This language is unfamiliar to most of our citizens, and likely to you. With guidance focused on introducing the mind of the composer to yours, your inner ear

---

1. The opening lines of Franz Schober's poem *An die Musik (To Music)*. The word *holde* is translated many ways, partly in respect to context. Kindly, beloved, noble would also fit here.

finds a welcome companion. Consider this: If you should find that you can indeed learn to follow the development of, say, a piano piece by Mozart or a song by Schubert, what does that say about your mind and that of the composer? And, if he composed his idea some 250 years ago, and through beauty inspires a higher power of thinking in you today, doesn't that suggest that he knew something profound about your mind?

Entertainment? Training?

In the early 1970s, it was no accident that Lyndon LaRouche came under direct threat to his life from powerful international circles just when he was engaged in publishing ground-breaking papers on the human mind, while his movement was growing rapidly. The focus of this work, coherent and intimately interwoven with his earlier, fundamental advance in economics, centered on creativity— creativity as the distinction of the human mind. As he had emphasized in previous work, creativity, properly (as opposed to popularly) understood, recognizes no essential difference between artistic and scientific domains. Contrary to the notion long promulgated by the European oligarchy, that an unbridgeable gap divides science from the arts; and diametrically opposed also to the prevailing nonsense that science comes down to nothing but elaborations of mathematics, LaRouche advanced in a new way the Classical recognition of mind that most directly threatens oligarchy. How does it threaten? Because the principle of oligarchy rests on the notion that a small elite is born to govern the mass of humanity; that the masses are unable, biologically, to rule themselves: they are naturally too stupid—never mind that oligarchies, generation to generation, have expended vast effort and treasure, just as they are doing now, to prevent whole populations from recognizing and developing their own true humanity.

Thus, LaRouche elucidated on a higher plane the essential republican principle of an educated, cultured citizenry participating in shaping its own future. He located the source of this in the human individual's natural potential for making willfully creative, valid new discoveries toward that end. For humanity, he demonstrated, what is normal, and fundamentally so, is creativity. In a sane society, scientific and technological revolution is complimented by expressions in art which celebrate the same creative process through which such progress is achieved. Not every scientist may become an Einstein, not every artist a Leonardo or Beethoven; nor is every person by profession a scientist or artist— but, every member of society may appreciate that standard and participate meaningfully in some way!

LaRouche's unwanted, bold assertion about normalcy, combined with his policy initiatives on global economic development, compounded his established audacity in publicly shredding the "scientific" veneer of a coordinated new wave of frauds designed to undermine and reverse the potentials of, particularly, the more advanced nations. The late 1960s' new calculation of Malthusian "overpopulation," the radical environmentalist movement, and the new hedonism were just being fully launched. LaRouche was getting in the way, just as the Kennedys and Martin Luther King, Jr., and others, had earlier.

Over the more than forty years since then, LaRouche's forecasts of what those oligarchic policies spelled for humanity have been unerringly realized. But, if he, like Leonardo and Beethoven, was right about the mind, what does that imply for our ability to create a norm in society based on creativity?

An 1876 work by American painter Thomas Eakins offers an opening to one path toward an answer. "Baby at Play" (in the National Gallery of Art in Washington, D.C.), shows us a well-dressed, very young child playing outside on a brick path. In its hand is a square block at an angle to an intersection of bricks. Close by are

National Gallery of Art, Washington, DC

"Baby at Play" by American painter Thomas Eakins, 1876

creative commons/The Panhead

Popular music reflects today's culture in general, the one that burns. Perhaps it's smooth and quiet, or toe-tapping dance music, or violent and rageful. Here, the Christian rock group Skillet.

other blocks, of various shape and size, some balanced one on top of another. We see that other blocks have been placed in a little carriage drawn by a toy horse. After a time, we may notice a small doll that has been cast aside in the background. The sunlight from overhead casts the child's eyes into shadow, but the expression is concentrated, intense. This is not a casual or romanticized view of childhood, nor a portrait of one particular child. A problem is being solved.

Children naturally enjoy solving problems. Compare, though, today's popular toys, with their incorporation of unbridled rage getting its way in "action figures," games, and similar items.

Entertainment? Training?

Look again at Eakins' portrayal, and imagine the child growing into adulthood. Imagine yourself, enjoying a coherence between work and leisure; that rather than continually trying to escape from the wild vortices of the present, you were engaging in the process of creating a better future. The truth is, the very Classical arts you have been denied offer crucial nourishment for the capacity for self-development. The key lies in bringing yourself to recognize the intrinsic connection of the fight for our just economic and political future, to that for a return to normal human qualities in the arts. These two now seemingly disconnected pursuits are but features of a single cultural paradigm. We see it, for example, reflected in the Florentine Renaissance—following a hideous dark age—in which cities were designed to surround a population with beauty; in the organically ordered, self-developing design of buildings, the proportioned public spaces featuring sculptures and relief art, and of course the great revolutions in language and painting, leading into the flowering of the arts which followed. Today, that paradigm has all but vanished under a century-long assault, an attack on a growing population increasingly better educated to participate in the mission of improving life for all mankind, here on Earth now and venturing increasingly into the galaxy. Today's paradigm, with its pervasive glorification of irrationality, coheres only with a population dumbed-down, and "entertained" by sensuality, threat, and violence, accompanied incessantly by the beat, the beat, the beat of a music kindled by those who reveled in reducing humanity to a beastlike existence.

"But wait," you protest. "I'm all for economic progress and better education, but you can't take my music away!" You're right. No one can take it away from you; you carry it inside. But the silent principle upon which degenerate music is based, is one irreconcilably opposed to what is most human about you, to what is, in truth, most normal. What future shall we build by respecting a violation of our humanity?

The Classical in art is the friend of every person. It seeks, through countless forms in numerous languages—architecture, drawing, music, photography, poetry and drama, sculpture—to enliven the creative spark in those who experience it, by presenting lawful ironies for them to resolve, just as, for the good scientist, anomalies, paradoxes between current theory and experimental evidence, present problems to be solved creatively. Good art may choose the humor of life as well as its struggles and tragedies, but holds within it a reflection of creative reason, that it may impart something of universal value to add to the lives of those it touches. Thus it reminds us of what, really, we are.

Escape from reality? The time is grown too dark already; let us descend no further into an age of barbarity. Drawing from the wealth of beauty in Classical art, unfamiliar though it be, we may begin to understand what we have been robbed of, and begin to create a new renaissance in which, at last, true scientific and artistic creativity may, as normal, take its proper place.

Du holde Kunst, ich danke dir! *You noble art, I thank you!*